MAR 1 0 2014

D0874664

✦ NEW ✦
CLASSIC
PATCH
WORK

New Classic Patchwork
First published in the United States in 2014 by Interweave

INTERWEAVE.
interweave.com

Interweave
A division of F+W Media, Inc.
201 East Fourth Street
Loveland, CO 80537
interweave.com

All rights reserved. The written instructions, photographs, designs, patterns and projects
in this volume are intended for the personal use of the reader and may be reproduced for
that purpose only. Any other use, especially commercial use, is forbidden under law
without the express written permission of the copyright holder. Violators will be prosecuted
to the fullest extent of the law. No other part of this book may be reproduced in any form
or by any electronic or mechanical means including information storage and retrieval
systems without permission in writing from the original publisher, except by a reviewer,
who may quote a brief passage in review.

The information in this book was originally published in the Japanese language by Nihon Vogue Co., LTD.
in the following title:
YOKO SAITO NO PACCHIWAAKU ORIJINARU DEZAIN 156
156 Original Patchwork Designs by Yoko Saito
Copyright © Yoko Saito / NIHON VOGUE-SHA 2005
English language rights, translation & production by World Book Media, LLC
Email: info@worldbookmedia.com

Photography: Akinori Miyashita, Kana Watanabe
Translation: Kyoko Matthews
English-language editor: Lindsay Fair

Library of Congress
Cataloging-in-Publication Data not available at time of printing

ISBN-13: 978-1-62033-533-8

Printed in China
10 9 8 7 6 5 4 3 2 1

NEW CLASSIC PATCH WORK

YOKO SAITO

78 original motifs and **10** projects

WILLARD LIBRARY, BATTLE CREEK, MI

CONTENTS

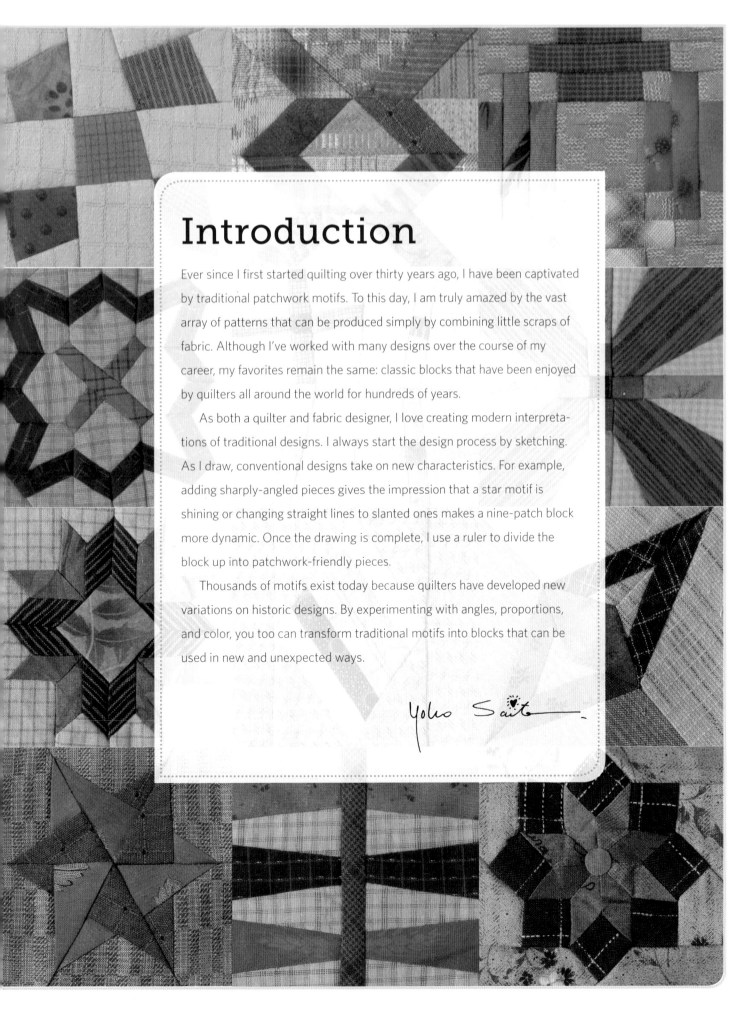

Introduction

Ever since I first started quilting over thirty years ago, I have been captivated by traditional patchwork motifs. To this day, I am truly amazed by the vast array of patterns that can be produced simply by combining little scraps of fabric. Although I've worked with many designs over the course of my career, my favorites remain the same: classic blocks that have been enjoyed by quilters all around the world for hundreds of years.

As both a quilter and fabric designer, I love creating modern interpretations of traditional designs. I always start the design process by sketching. As I draw, conventional designs take on new characteristics. For example, adding sharply-angled pieces gives the impression that a star motif is shining or changing straight lines to slanted ones makes a nine-patch block more dynamic. Once the drawing is complete, I use a ruler to divide the block up into patchwork-friendly pieces.

Thousands of motifs exist today because quilters have developed new variations on historic designs. By experimenting with angles, proportions, and color, you too can transform traditional motifs into blocks that can be used in new and unexpected ways.

Yoko Saito

How to Use This Book

Each block design includes a full-size photograph, a template, and a construction steps diagram. To make a block, cut out all the patchwork pieces, then sew the pieces together following the process illustrated by the construction steps. The following guide shows you how the block instructions are formatted in this book and includes some general tips for creating the blocks.

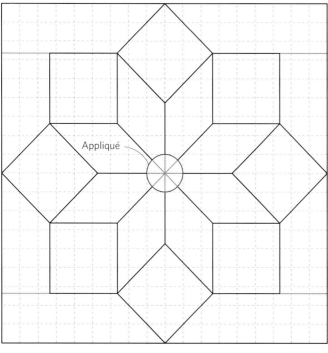

SELECTING YOUR FABRIC

✤ Scrap fabric is used for all blocks, so the block instructions do not include a materials list.

✤ The photographs of each block are full-size, excluding seam allowances. The finished size for most blocks is a 3½" (9 cm) square.

The designs in this book were created using metric measurements. Any measurements noted in inches within the book are conversions of the metric measurements. For the greatest accuracy, use the metric version of all measurements.

CUTTING THE BLOCKS

✤ The templates in this book are full-size, unless otherwise noted. Using the full-size templates will produce 3½" (9 cm) square finished blocks. A handful of the templates will need to be enlarged 200%. For best results, use a photocopier to enlarge the templates.

✤ The templates can be enlarged or reduced as desired. Each template is printed on a grid of ³⁄₁₆" (0.5 cm) squares. Use this measurement as your scale when resizing.

✤ The templates do not include seam allowance. When cutting your fabric, add ¼" (0.6 cm) seam allowance around each patchwork piece.

✤ When adjacent patchwork pieces are divided with a gray line on the template, use the same fabric for both pieces.

✤ Pink lines on the block template indicate appliqué.

CONSTRUCTION STEPS

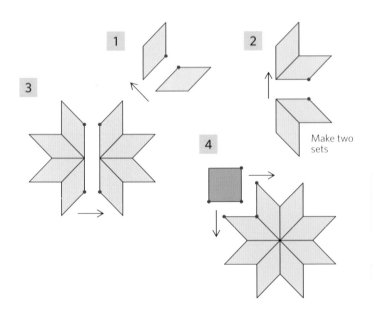

SEWING FROM EDGE TO EDGE

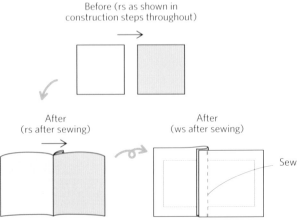

Sew from edge to edge and press the seam allowance in the direction indicated by the arrow.

SEWING THE BLOCKS

- All of the blocks in this book are created with basic patchwork sewing. Some of the blocks also incorporate appliqué, which is done after the block has been pieced together.
- The numbers indicate the order in which the patchwork pieces are sewn together to form the block. Follow the recommended sewing order for best results.
- Always sew with ¼" (0.6 cm) seam allowance, unless otherwise noted.
- Unless otherwise noted, sew the patchwork pieces together from edge to edge. Backstitch at both the beginning and end of each seam.
- The red dots indicate to start or stop sewing at the seam allowance, rather than from edge to edge. This technique is used to set pieces into each other.
- The arrows indicate the direction to press the seam allowance. The seam allowance should always be pressed in the direction that makes it least visible from the right side. Use the arrows as a guide; however, you may need to make adjustments based on the color or thickness of your fabric.

USING THE RED DOTS:
How to Start and Stop Sewing at the Seam Allowance

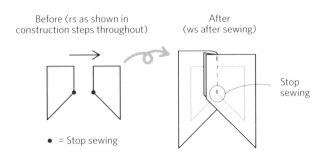

Stop sewing at the red dot and press the seam allowance in the direction indicated by the arrow. Seam allowance will not be pictured in the construction steps.

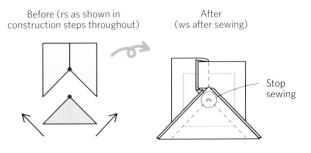

1 Freestyle Nine-Patch

Full of sharp angles and slanted lines, this block offers a fresh interpretation of the traditional nine-patch motif. I chose a symmetrical, grid-like print as the background fabric to emphasize the freestyle shape of the patchwork pieces and create contrast.

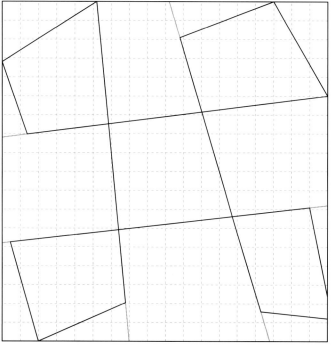

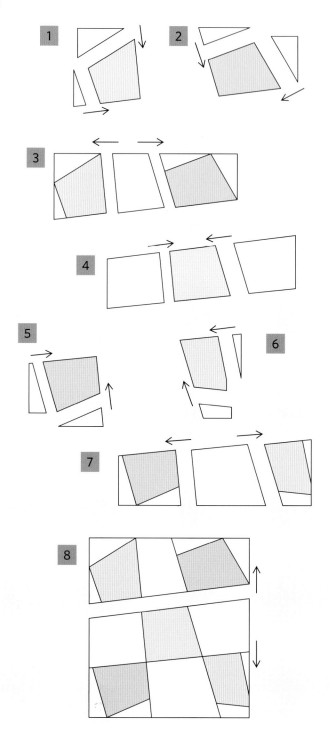

» When cutting your fabric, add ¼" (0.6 cm) seam allowance around each patchwork piece.

» When adjacent pieces are divided with a gray line, use the same fabric.

» Always press the seam allowances in the direction indicated by the arrows.

CONSTRUCTION STEPS

1

2

4

3

Align

5

6

7

8

9

2 Parallel Cross

This contemporary block was inspired by the number symbol—a character we use everyday on our telephones and computers. I love the effect created by fashioning a modern symbol out of traditional, home-spun fabrics. Use a uniform background fabric and center the design to make the unique shape the center of attention in this block.

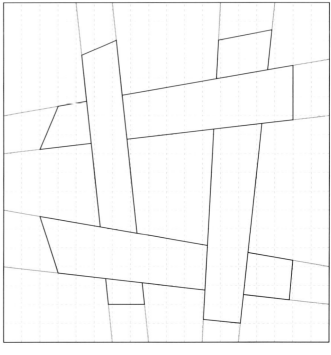

» When cutting your fabric, add ¼" (0.6 cm) seam allowance around each patchwork piece.

» When adjacent pieces are divided with a gray line, use the same fabric.

» Always press the seam allowances in the direction indicated by the arrows.

» The • marks to stop sewing at the seam allowance.

3 Old Well

The appearance of this block can be totally transformed based upon your fabric choice. Use one fabric for both the inner frame and outer lines, as pictured here, or use two different fabrics to make the frame look as if it is sitting on top of the lines. This motif is a quilting optical illusion!

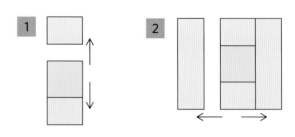

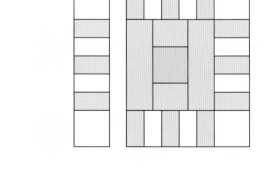

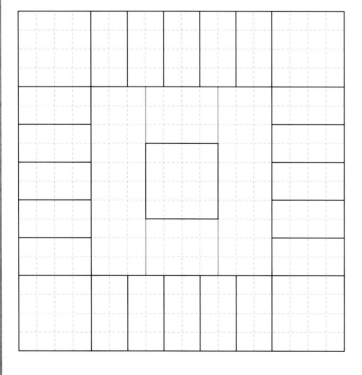

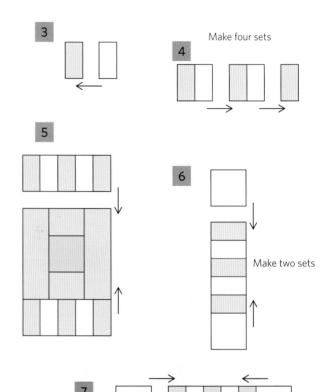

» When cutting your fabric, add ¼" (0.6 cm) seam allowance around each patchwork piece.
» When adjacent pieces are divided with a gray line, use the same fabric.
» Always press the seam allowances in the direction indicated by the arrows.

CONSTRUCTION STEPS

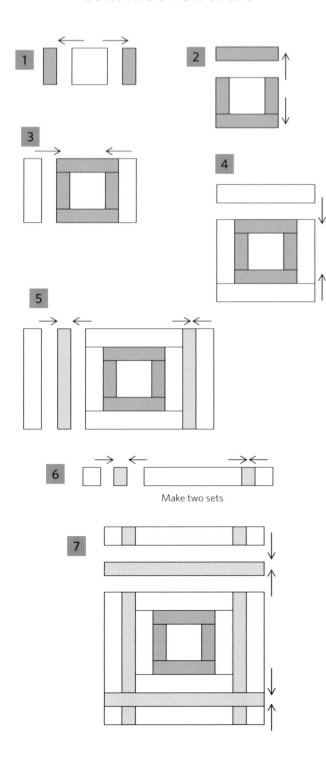

4 View Down a Well

I experimented with the concepts of perspective and depth when designing this block. By layering square frames of different widths and colors, I was able to achieve the effect of peering down a deep well. For maximum impact, choose fabrics within the same color family.

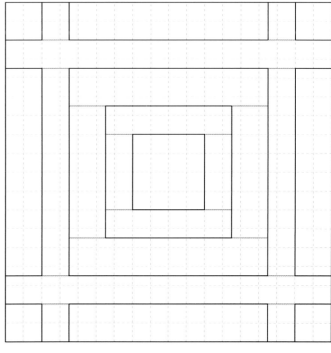

» When cutting your fabric, add ¼" (0.6 cm) seam allowance around each patchwork piece.

» When adjacent pieces are divided with a gray line, use the same fabric.

» Always press the seam allowances in the direction indicated by the arrows.

Make two sets

5 Hammering Pegs

This design is reminiscent of pegs being driven into the four sides of a wooden square. To make the "pegs" stand out, select fabrics that contrast with the block background, but still work well together.

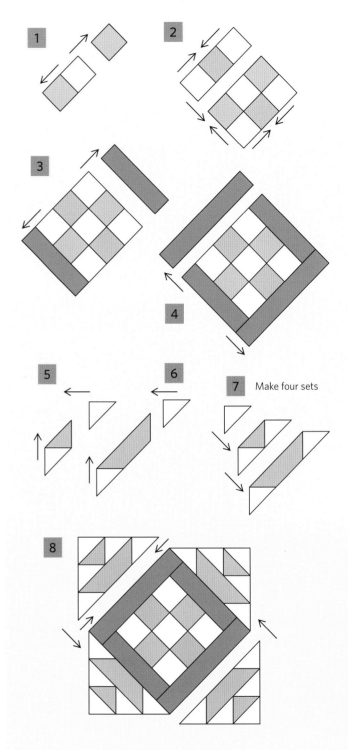

7 Make four sets

» When cutting your fabric, add ¼" (0.6 cm) seam allowance around each patchwork piece.

» When adjacent pieces are divided with a gray line, use the same fabric.

» Always press the seam allowances in the direction indicated by the arrows.

CONSTRUCTION STEPS

1

2

3

4

5

6

Make two sets

7

» When cutting your fabric, add ¼" (0.6 cm) seam allowance around each patchwork piece.

» When adjacent pieces are divided with a gray line, use the same fabric.

» Always press the seam allowances in the direction indicated by the arrows.

6 Zigzag Sandwich

The linear nature of this motif makes it well-suited for quilt borders. Piece several of these blocks together in both vertical and horizontal repeats to make an ornate frame for your quilt. Only you will know how quick and easy it was to make!

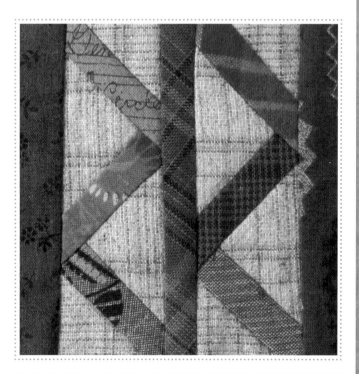

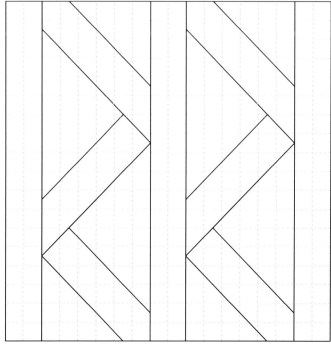

7 Cobra Dance

Although it makes a great border, this motif is spectacular in its own right. Play with your fabric selection to highlight the diamond pattern that appears when the zigzag lines connect. In the block pictured here, I created a background from several beige scraps, all featuring different patterns, for a truly dynamic design.

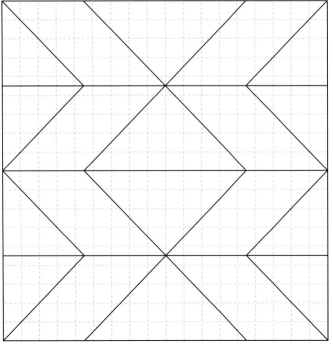

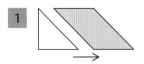

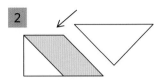

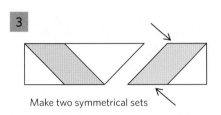

Make two symmetrical sets

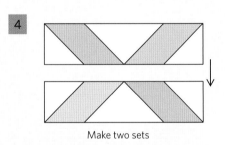

Make two sets

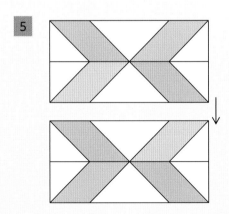

» When cutting your fabric, add ¼" (0.6 cm) seam allowance around each patchwork piece.
» When adjacent pieces are divided with a gray line, use the same fabric.
» Always press the seam allowances in the direction indicated by the arrows.

CONSTRUCTION STEPS

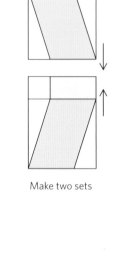

1

2

Make four symmetrical sets
(see diagram)

3 Make two sets

4 Make two sets

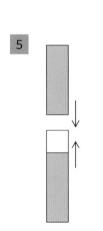

5

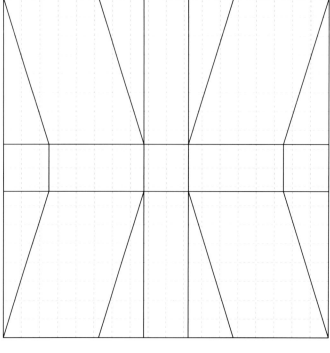

6

» When cutting your fabric, add ¼" (0.6 cm) seam allowance around each patchwork piece.

» When adjacent pieces are divided with a gray line, use the same fabric.

» Always press the seam allowances in the direction indicated by the arrows.

Combine repeats of this versatile block to create a number of interesting linear patterns. Stack the blocks vertically for a bold border design, or rotate them to produce a gentle zigzag, as used in the Zigzag Basket on page 16.

Zigzag Basket

This basket is the perfect size for storing everyday items that often clutter table tops, such as mail, keys, and spare change. This project is made by joining five **Tie a Sash** blocks to create horizontal zigzags. For a special touch, use fine wale corduroy for the handle, piping, and bottom. The corduroy provides the basket with a soft look and feel, all the while increasing durability!

Instructions on page 17

MATERIALS FOR ZIGZAG BASKET

Patchwork fabric: Assorted scraps

Accent fabric: 11¾" × 15¾" (30 × 40 cm) green corduroy fabric

Handle fabric: One 2" × 9¾" (5 × 25 cm) brown print fabric bias strip

Backing fabric: 13¾" × 19¾" (35 × 50 cm)

Lining fabric: 13¾" × 19¾" (35 × 50 cm)

Batting: 13¾" × 19¾" (35 × 50 cm)

Heavyweight fusible interfacing: 13¾" × 19¾" (35 × 50 cm)

Fusible interfacing: 1⅜" × 7⅞" (3.5 × 20 cm)

Piping: One 1" × 19¾" (2.5 × 50 cm) green corduroy fabric bias strip

Piping cord: 19¾" (50 cm) of ⅛" (0.3 cm) diameter cord

CUTTING INSTRUCTIONS

Seam allowance is not included. Add ¼" (0.6 cm) seam allowance to all piece edges.

Trace and cut out the Block #8 template on page 15 and the template on Pattern Sheet A. Cut out the pieces following the instructions listed on the templates.

Cut out the following pieces, which do not have templates, according to the measurements below:

» **Handle center:** ⅞" × 7⅞" (2.3 × 20 cm) of handle fabric
» **Handle borders (cut 2 on the bias):** 7/16" × 7⅞" (1.2 × 20 cm) of accent fabric
» **Handle lining (cut on the bias):** 1⅜" × 7⅞" (3.5 × 20 cm) of accent fabric
» **Handle interfacing (cut without seam allowance):** 1⅜" × 7⅞" (3.5 × 20 cm) of fusible interfacing

LAYOUT DIAGRAM

TOP

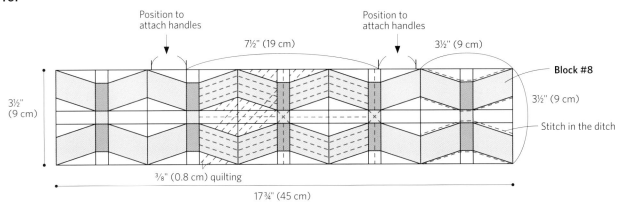

Position to attach handles

Position to attach handles

7½" (19 cm)

3½" (9 cm)

Block #8

3½" (9 cm)

3½" (9 cm)

Stitch in the ditch

⅜" (0.8 cm) quilting

17¾" (45 cm)

BOTTOM

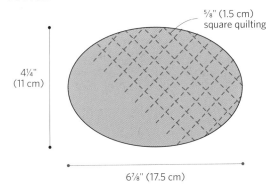

⅝" (1.5 cm) square quilting

4¼" (11 cm)

6⅞" (17.5 cm)

HANDLE

¼" (0.6 cm)

Quilting

1⅜" (3.5 cm)

7⅞" (20 cm)

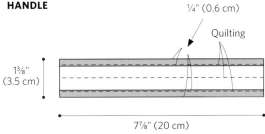

* Stitch in the ditch along all patchwork pieces.

* Sew using ¼" (0.6 cm) seam allowance, unless otherwise noted.

MAKE THE HANDLE

1. Adhere the fusible interfacing to the wrong side of the handle lining.

2. With right sides together, sew a handle border to each long edge of the handle center.

3. Align the handle lining, handle, and batting with right sides together and sew along long edges. Turn right side out.

4. Quilt, as shown in the Layout Diagram on page 18.

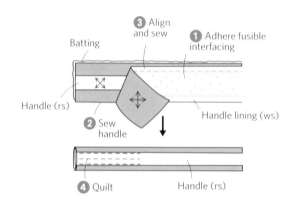

MAKE THE BASKET

1. Follow the instructions on page 15 to make five of Block #8. Sew the blocks together to make the top.

2. Cut the batting and backing slightly larger than the assembled top. Layer the top, batting, and backing. Baste. Quilt, as shown in the Layout Diagram on page 18.

3. With right sides together, sew the basket into a loop. Press the seam allowance open.

4. Fold the piping bias strip in half with the piping cord sandwiched in between. Sew the bias strip close to the cord using a 1/8" (0.3 cm) seam allowance.

5. Align the piping and handle with the basket along the opening edge. Baste. Make sure to baste both short ends of the handle to the basket.

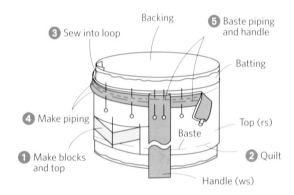

MAKE THE LINING

1. Adhere the heavyweight fusible interfacing to the wrong side of the lining.

2. With right sides together, sew the lining into a loop. Press the seam allowance open.

3. Align the basket and lining with right sides together and sew along the opening edge.

4. Trim the excess seam allowance. Turn the lining to the inside of the basket.

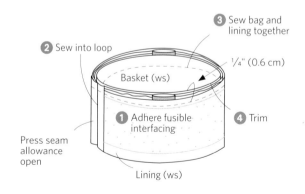

MAKE THE BOTTOM

1. Cut the batting and bottom foundation slightly larger than the bottom. Adhere the heavyweight fusible interfacing to the wrong side of the bottom foundation.

2. Layer the bottom, batting, and bottom foundation. Baste. Quilt, as shown in the Layout Diagram on page 18.

3. Running stitch along the bottom of the basket. Leave long thread tails. Pull the thread tails to gather the basket into shape.

4. Baste the bottom to the basket.

5. Adhere the heavyweight fusible interfacing to the wrong side of the bottom lining.

6. Running stitch along the bottom lining. Leave long thread tails. Pull the thread tails to gather the bottom lining into shape.

7. Slip-stitch the bottom lining to the basket lining.

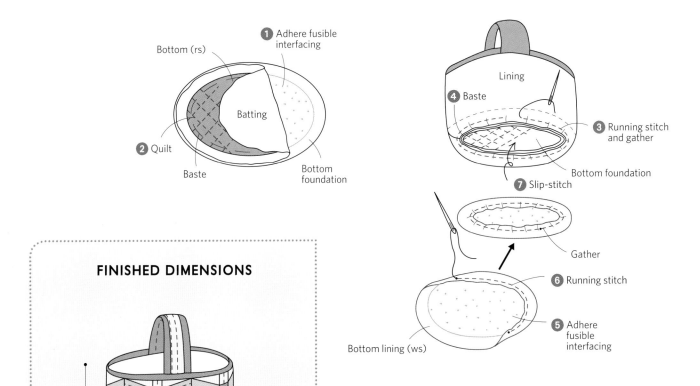

FINISHED DIMENSIONS

3⅝" (9.3 cm)

4¼" (11 cm)

6⅞" (17.5 cm)

CONSTRUCTION STEPS

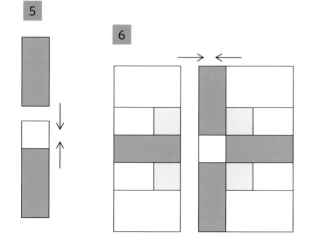

1

2

Make four symmetrical
sets (see diagram)

3

4

Make two sets

5

6

» When cutting your fabric, add ¼" (0.6 cm) seam
allowance around each patchwork piece.
» When adjacent pieces are divided with a gray line,
use the same fabric.
» Always press the seam allowances in the direction
indicated by the arrows.

9 Crossroads

I received a pleasant surprise when I pieced several of these
blocks together: the resulting pattern resembled a city from a
bird's-eye view! The thick black fabric strips are reminiscent
of streets intersecting and extending in every direction. As
a fun touch, I fussy cut a floral print for the block's central
square.

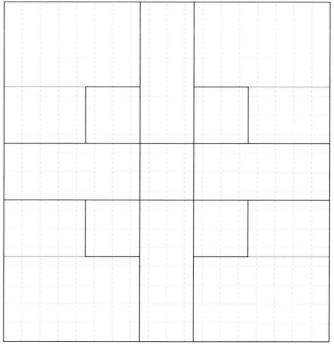

10 Rectangle Window

The dark square frame and colorful vertical rectangles featured in this design remind me of a stained glass window. I used a strong color for the square frame and corner triangles to anchor the block. This motif also works well when rotated 90°.

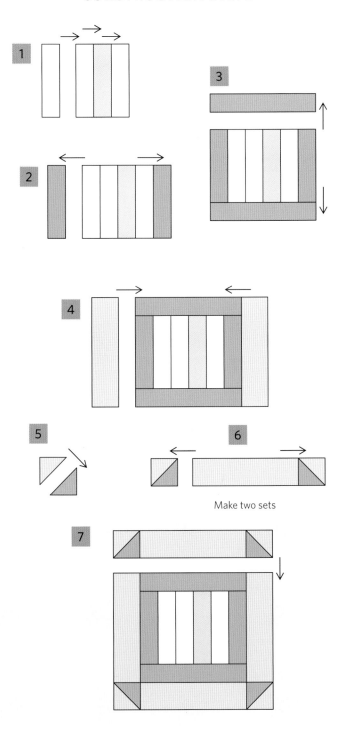

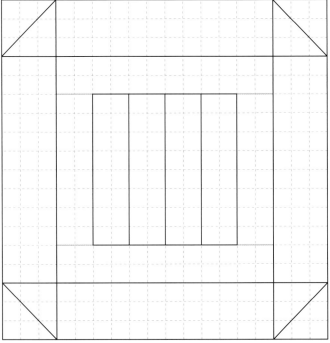

» When cutting your fabric, add ¼" (0.6 cm) seam allowance around each patchwork piece.
» When adjacent pieces are divided with a gray line, use the same fabric.
» Always press the seam allowances in the direction indicated by the arrows.

CONSTRUCTION STEPS

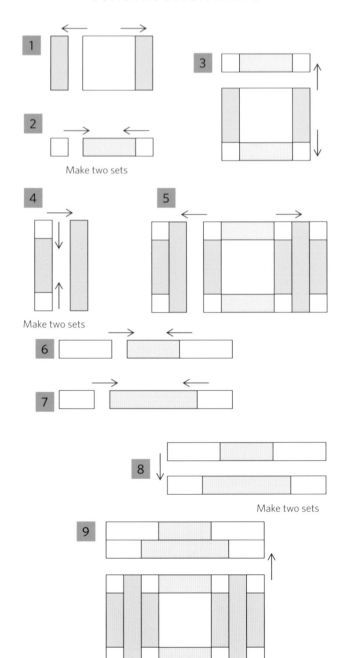

Make two sets

Make two sets

Make two sets

11 Parquet Party

For this block, several rectangles and squares of equal width are combined in a mosaic-like pattern reminiscent of a wooden parquet floor. To change up the look of this block, use the same fabric for opposing motifs, as illustrated in the construction steps.

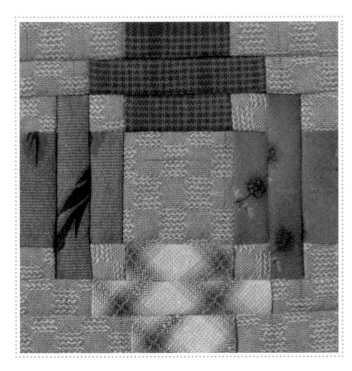

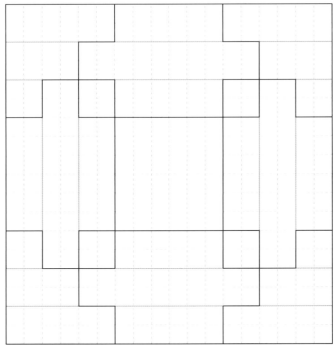

» When cutting your fabric, add ¼" (0.6 cm) seam allowance around each patchwork piece.

» When adjacent pieces are divided with a gray line, use the same fabric.

» Always press the seam allowances in the direction indicated by the arrows.

12 Labyrinth

This block may appear complicated, but it's actually very simple to sew. To create this maze-inspired design, alternate between colored fabric and a neutral background fabric to form L-shaped strips within each row. Choose the center square fabric carefully as different colors will change the look and feel of the block.

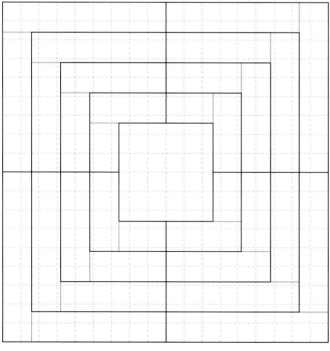

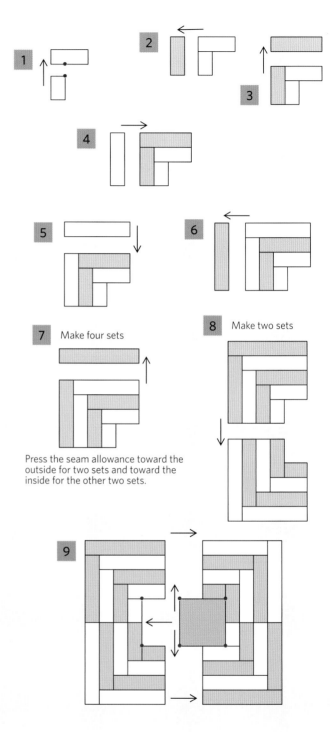

7 Make four sets

Press the seam allowance toward the outside for two sets and toward the inside for the other two sets.

8 Make two sets

» When cutting your fabric, add ¼" (0.6 cm) seam allowance around each patchwork piece.

» When adjacent pieces are divided with a gray line, use the same fabric.

» Always press the seam allowances in the direction indicated by the arrows.

» The • marks to stop sewing at the seam allowance.

CONSTRUCTION STEPS

1

2

3 Make two sets

Press seam allowances up
for one set and down for the
other set.

4

» When cutting your fabric, add ¼" (0.6 cm) seam
allowance around each patchwork piece.

» When adjacent pieces are divided with a gray line,
use the same fabric.

» Always press the seam allowances in the direction
indicated by the arrows.

13 Taupe Color Study

I truly enjoy selecting fabric for basic geometric blocks
because their simple design puts the focus on color, pattern,
and texture. This bold motif, used in the Taupe Study Tote
on page 26, provides an excellent opportunity to experiment
with contrast.

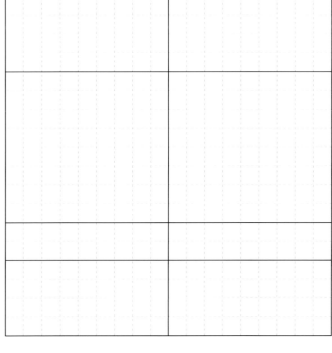

Taupe Study Tote

This tote uses six **Taupe Color Study** blocks to create a front pocket that runs the length of the entire bag. Can you tell where one block ends and the next begins? Here's a hint: I omitted the top row for three of the blocks. I love the idea of using only a portion of a block in order to make the design look continuous.

Instructions on page 27

MATERIALS FOR TAUPE STUDY TOTE

Patchwork fabric: Assorted scraps

Main fabric: 13¾" × 19¾" (35 × 50 cm) dark brown woven

Accent fabric: 9¾" × 13¾" (25 × 35 cm) dark brown plaid

Gusset fabric: Two 2" × 7⅞" (5 × 20 cm) golden brown plaids

Bottom/gusset pocket fabric: 7⅞" × 21¾" (20 × 55 cm) black plaid

Backing: 35½" × 43¼" (90 × 110 cm)

Batting: 35½" × 43¼" (90 × 110 cm)

Binding:

> **For pocket openings and gusset:** Two 1⅜" × 35½" (3.5 × 90 cm) black plaid bias strips

> **For bottom/gusset pocket:** One 1⅜" × 11¾" (3.5 × 30 cm) light brown plaid bias strip

For seam allowances: One 1³⁄₁₆" × 55⅛" (3 × 140 cm) bias strip

Double-sided fusible interfacing: 8¼" × 10⅝" (21 × 27 cm)

Fusible interfacing: 11¾" × 29½" (30 × 75 cm)

Zipper: One 12" (30.5 cm) long zipper

Handle: One set of 5³⁄₁₆" (13.2 cm) long leather handles with metal fasteners

Cord: 6" (15 cm) of ¹⁄₃₂" (0.1 cm) diameter cord

Beads: Two wooden beads

CUTTING INSTRUCTIONS

Seam allowance is not included. Add ¼" (0.6 cm) seam allowance to all piece edges.

Trace and cut out the Block #13 template on page 25. Cut out the pieces.

Cut out the following pieces, which do not have templates, according to the measurements below:

» **Front:** 8¼" × 10⅝" (21 × 27 cm) of main fabric

» **A:** 2" × 10⅝" (5 × 27 cm) of main fabric

» **B:** 6¼" × 10⅝" (16 × 27 cm) of accent fabric

» **Back pocket linings (cut 2):** 8¼" × 10⅝" (21 × 27 cm) of backing fabric

» **Back pocket lining interfacing (cut without seam allowance):** 8¼" × 10⅝" (21 × 27 cm) of double-sided fusible interfacing

» **Gusset top (cut 2):** 2" × 4" (5 × 10 cm) of main fabric

» **Gusset bottom (cut 2):** 4" × 5¾" (10 × 14.5 cm) of gusset fabric

» **Gusset interfacing (cut 2 without seam allowance):** 4" × 7¾" (10 × 19.5 cm) of fusible interfacing

» **Bottom/gusset pocket:** 4" × 18⅞" (10 × 47.9 cm) of bottom/gusset pocket fabric

» **Bottom/gusset pocket interfacing (cut without seam allowance):** 4" × 18⅞" (10 × 47.9 cm) of fusible interfacing

» **Facing:** 1⁹⁄₁₆" × 29⅛" (4 × 74 cm) of backing fabric

» **Facing interfacing (cut without seam allowance):** 1⁹⁄₁₆" × 29⅛" (4 × 74 cm) of fusible interfacing

LAYOUT DIAGRAM

FRONT POCKET

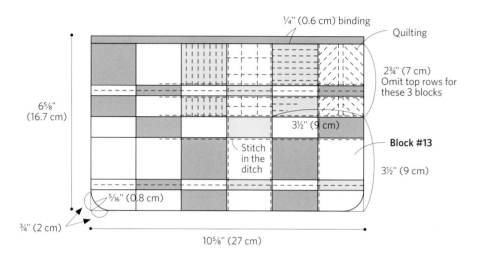

¼" (0.6 cm) binding

Quilting

2¾" (7 cm)
Omit top rows for
these 3 blocks

6⅝"
(16.7 cm)

3½" (9 cm)

Block #13

3½" (9 cm)

Stitch
in the
ditch

⁵⁄₁₆" (0.8 cm)

¾" (2 cm)

10⅝" (27 cm)

FRONT

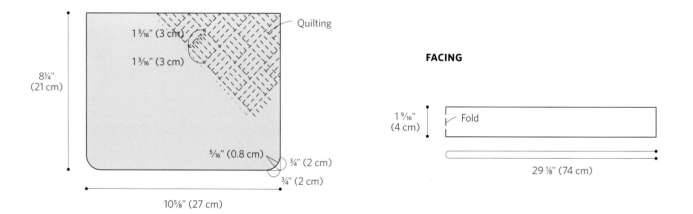

Quilting

1³⁄₁₆" (3 cm)

1³⁄₁₆" (3 cm)

8¼"
(21 cm)

⁵⁄₁₆" (0.8 cm)

¾" (2 cm)

¾" (2 cm)

10⅝" (27 cm)

FACING

1⁹⁄₁₆"
(4 cm)

Fold

29⅛" (74 cm)

BACK

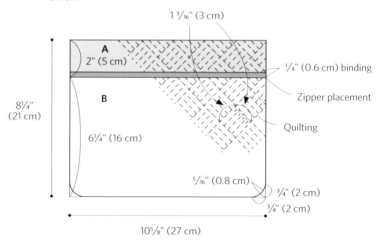

1 ³/₁₆" (3 cm)

A
2" (5 cm)

¼" (0.6 cm) binding

Zipper placement

Quilting

B

8¼"
(21 cm)

6¼" (16 cm)

⁵/₁₆" (0.8 cm)

¾" (2 cm)

¾" (2 cm)

10⁵/₈" (27 cm)

GUSSET (cut 2)

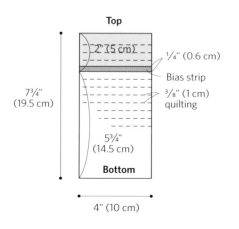

Top

2" (5 cm)

¼" (0.6 cm)

Bias strip

7¾"
(19.5 cm)

³/₈" (1 cm)
quilting

5¾"
(14.5 cm)

Bottom

4" (10 cm)

BOTTOM/GUSSET POCKET

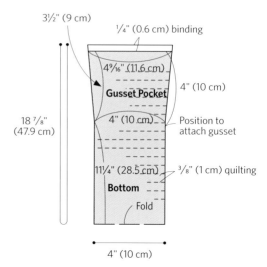

3½" (9 cm)

¼" (0.6 cm) binding

4⁹/₁₆" (11.6 cm)

4" (10 cm)

Gusset Pocket

4" (10 cm)

Position to
attach gusset

18 ⁷/₈"
(47.9 cm)

11¼" (28.5 cm)

³/₈" (1 cm) quilting

Bottom

Fold

4" (10 cm)

> » Stitch in the ditch around all patchwork pieces.
> » Sew using ¼" (0.6 cm) seam allowance, unless
>   otherwise noted.

MAKE THE FRONT

1 Follow the instructions on page 25 to make six of Block #13 (omit the top row for three blocks). To make the front pocket top, sew the blocks together in two rows of three.

2 Cut the batting and backing slightly larger than the assembled front pocket top. Layer the front pocket top, batting, and backing. Baste, then quilt, as shown in the Layout Diagram on page 28.

3 Bind the upper edge of the front pocket with the bias strip.

4 Cut the batting and backing slightly larger than the front. Layer the front, batting, and backing. Quilt, as shown in the Layout Diagram on page 28.

5 Layer the front pocket and the front. Baste together around the outer edges.

6 Sew the pocket divider seam, stitching through all layers.

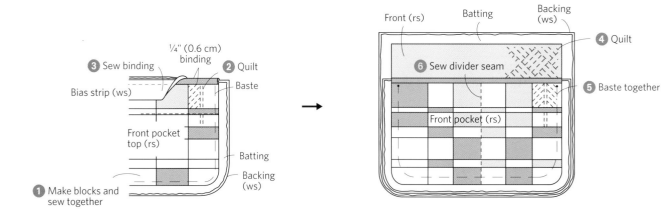

MAKE THE BACK

1. Cut the batting and backing slightly larger than A. Layer A, batting, and backing. Baste, then quilt, as shown in the Layout Diagram on page 29.

2. Bind the lower edge of A.

3. Repeat step 1 for B.

4. With right sides together, sew one side of the zipper to B. Trim the excess seam allowances and excess zipper length, if necessary. Fold the zipper seam allowance under and slip-stitch to the backing. Repeat to attach the other side of the zipper to A.

5. Adhere double-sided fusible interfacing to the wrong sides of the back pocket linings.

6. Align the back pocket linings and the back. Baste together around the outer edges.

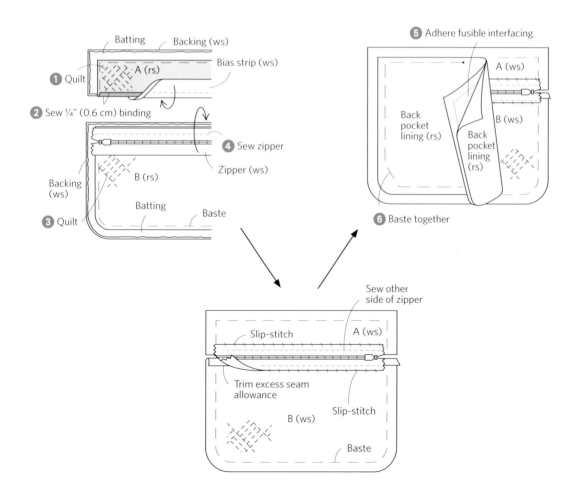

MAKE THE GUSSET

1. Sew the bias strip between the gusset top and bottom.

2. Cut the batting and backing slightly larger than assembled gusset. Adhere fusible interfacing to the wrong side of the gusset backing. Layer the gusset, batting, and backing. Baste, then quilt, as shown in the Layout Diagram on page 29.

3. Repeat steps 1 and 2 to make another gusset.

4. Follow step 2 to make the bottom/gusset pocket.

5. Bind the short edges of the bottom/gusset pocket.

6. Align the bottom/gusset pocket so it covers about half of the gusset. Topstitch to sew the two pieces together along the lower edge of the gusset.

7. Trim the seam allowances, except the gusset backing seam allowance. Wrap the gusset backing seam allowances around the trimmed seam allowances and slip-stitch.

8. Baste the gusset and bottom/gusset pocket together along the overlapped portion.

9. Repeat steps 5-8 with the other gusset.

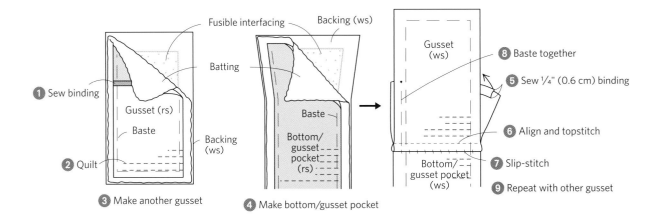

SEW THE BAG TOGETHER

1. With right sides together, sew the assembled gusset to the front and back.

2. Bind the seam allowances with the bias strip.

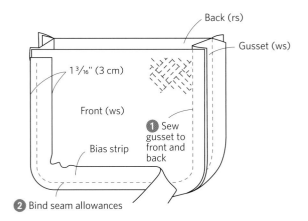

MAKE THE FACING

1 Adhere fusible interfacing to the wrong side of the facing.

2 Sew the short ends of the facing together to make a loop. Press the seam allowance open.

3 With right sides together, sew the facing to the bag opening.

4 Fold the facing to the inside and slip-stitch

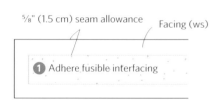

⅝" (1.5 cm) seam allowance · Facing (ws)

1 Adhere fusible interfacing

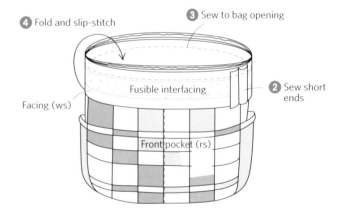

4 Fold and slip-stitch · **3** Sew to bag opening

Fusible interfacing

2 Sew short ends

Facing (ws)

Front pocket (rs)

ATTACH THE HANDLES

1 Make two holes on the front and two holes on the back to insert the handles. Make the holes through all layers. Insert the handles through the holes and secure on the inside of the bag using the metal fasteners.

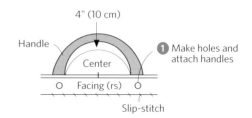

4" (10 cm)

Handle

Center

1 Make holes and attach handles

Facing (rs)

Slip-stitch

MAKE THE ZIPPER CHARM

1 Fold the cord in half and tie to the zipper pull. Thread the wooden beads onto the cord, then tie a knot.

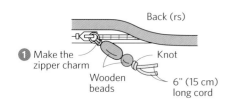

Back (rs)

1 Make the zipper charm

Knot

Wooden beads

6" (15 cm) long cord

FINISHED DIMENSIONS

8¼" (21 cm)

4" (10 cm)

10⅝" (27 cm)

14 Wood Stacks

Put your scrap pile to good use with this oversized motif, which is actually composed of four miniature blocks. The generous size of this block makes it perfect for large-scale projects, such as the Tailgate Tote on the opposite page.

Enlarge pattern 200%

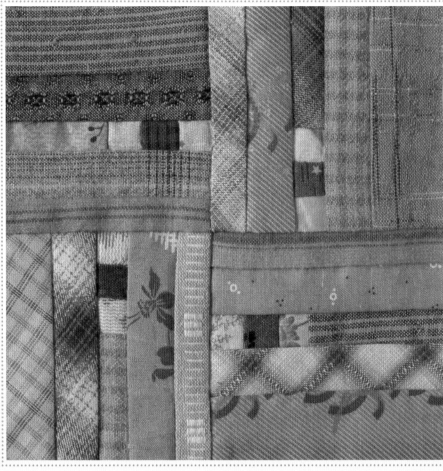

CONSTRUCTION STEPS

1

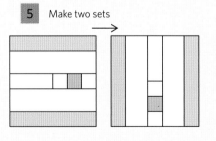

2

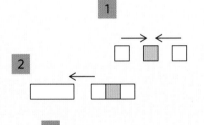

3

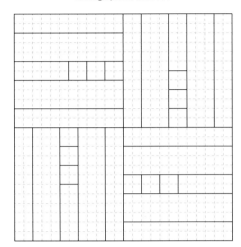

4 Make four sets

5 Make two sets

6

» When cutting your fabric, add ¼" (0.6 cm) seam allowance around each patchwork piece.

» When adjacent pieces are divided with a gray line, use the same fabric.

» Always press the seam allowances in the direction indicated by the arrows.

Tailgate Tote

The deep bucket-like shape of this tote is perfect for carrying wine bottles. It's made with the **Wood Stacks** block on page 34, which is essentially a scrap quilt block using a series of thin fabric strips sewn together. The bottom of the bag is constructed with multiple layers to add strength and durability for hauling your precious cargo.

Instructions on page 36

MATERIALS FOR TAILGATE TOTE

Patchwork fabric: Assorted scraps

Backing: 27½" × 39⅜" (70 × 100 cm)

Batting: 27½" × 39⅜" (70 × 100 cm)

Bottom fabric: 7⅞" × 7⅞" (20 × 20 cm)

Bottom foundation fabric: 7⅞" × 7⅞" (20 × 20 cm)

Binding: One 1³⁄₁₆" × 63" (3 × 160 cm) brown striped bias strip

Heavyweight fusible interfacing: 6" × 11¾" (15 × 30 cm)

Handles: One set of 1 ³⁄₁₆" × 11 ¾" (3 × 30 cm) nylon web handles

CUTTING INSTRUCTIONS

Seam allowance is not included. Add ¼" (0.6 cm) seam allowance to all piece edges.

Trace and cut out the Block #14 template on page 34. Cut out the pieces.

Cut out the following pieces, which do not have templates, according to the measurements below:

» **Bottom:** 5 ½" (14 cm) diameter circle of bottom fabric

» **Bottom foundation:** 5 ½" (14 cm) diameter circle of bottom foundation fabric

» **Bottom foundation interfacing (cut without seam allowance):** 5 ½" (14 cm) diameter circle of heavyweight fusible interfacing

» **Bottom batting:** 5 ½" (14 cm) diameter circle of batting

» **Bottom lining:** 5 ½" (14 cm) diameter circle of backing fabric

» **Bottom lining interfacing (cut without seam allowance):** 5 ½" (14 cm) diameter circle of heavyweight fusible interfacing

LAYOUT DIAGRAM

TOP (make 2)

1³⁄₁₆" (3 cm)

1³⁄₁₆" (3 cm) 14¼" (36 cm)

3½" (9 cm)

Position to attach handle

4¾" (12 cm)

Block #14

4¾" (12 cm)

14¼" (36 cm)

Quilting

8¾" (22 cm)

BOTTOM

³⁄₈" (1 cm) square quilting

5½" (14 cm)

MAKE THE TOPS AND SEW TOGETHER

1. Follow the instructions on page 34 to make 22 of Block #14. To make each top, sew eleven blocks together into two rows of four and one row of three.

2. Cut the batting and backing slightly larger than each assembled top. Layer each top, batting, and backing. Quilt, as shown in the Layout Diagram on page 36.

3. Make a template of the top using the dimensions in the Layout Diagram on page 36. Use the template to mark the finishing lines. Cut out the tops, leaving a large seam allowance.

4. With right sides together, sew the two tops along the sides.

5. Trim all seam allowances, except for one of the backings, to ¼" (0.6 cm).

6. On each side, wrap the backing seam allowance around the trimmed seam allowances and slip-stitch.

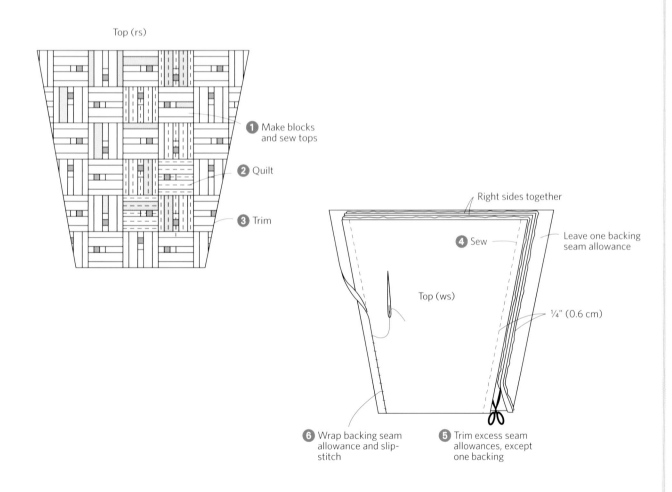

Top (rs)

1 Make blocks and sew tops

2 Quilt

3 Trim

Right sides together

4 Sew

Leave one backing seam allowance

Top (ws)

¼" (0.6 cm)

6 Wrap backing seam allowance and slip-stitch

5 Trim excess seam allowances, except one backing

MAKE THE BOTTOM

1. Adhere heavyweight fusible interfacing to the wrong side of the bottom foundation.

2. Layer bottom, batting, and bottom foundation. Baste.

3. Quilt with ⅜" (1 cm) squares, as shown in the Layout Diagram on page 36.

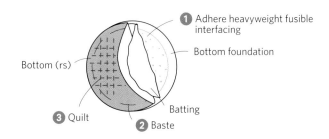

ATTACH THE BOTTOM TO THE BAG

1. Running stitch the bag along the bottom outline and gather into shape.

2. Align the bottom and the bag with right sides together and sew.

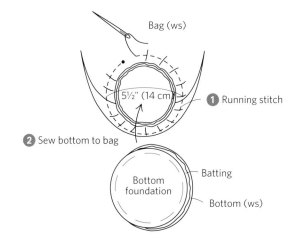

ATTACH THE BOTTOM LINING

1. Adhere heavyweight fusible interfacing to the wrong side of the bottom lining.

2. Running stitch the bottom lining and gather into shape.

3. Slip-stitch the bottom lining to the inside of the bag.

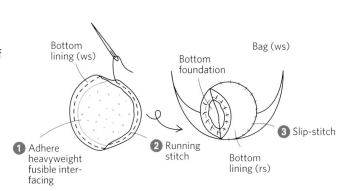

ATTACH THE HANDLES

1 With right sides together, sew two bias strips with handles sandwiched in between. Make sure the handles are positioned 8¼" (21 cm) apart.

2 Open and press flat.

3 Sew the short ends together to make a loop. Press seam allowance open.

4 With right sides together, sew the bias strip loop to the bag opening. Make sure the handles are positioned according to the Layout Diagram on page 36.

5 Wrap the bias strip around the seam allowances and slip-stitch to the inside of the bag.

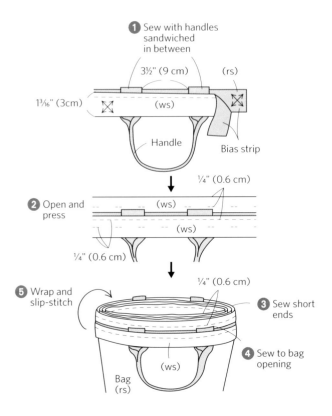

FINISHED DIMENSIONS

15 Chessboard

Composed of several ⅜" (1 cm) squares, this block is another great stash buster. Use a different material for each square, or alternate between light and dark fabrics for a modern twist. I added a double border to frame this game board-inspired design.

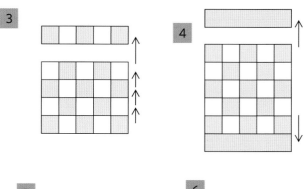

Make three sets

Make two sets

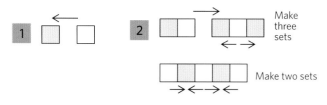

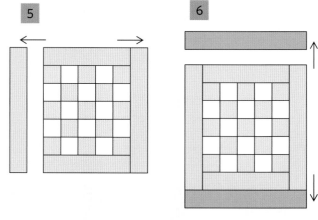

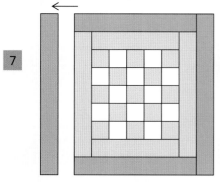

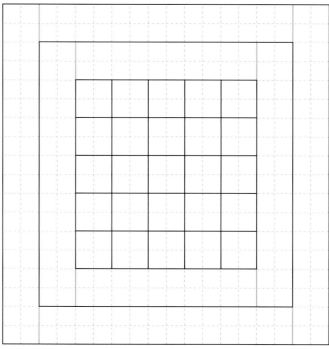

» When cutting your fabric, add ¼" (0.6 cm) seam allowance around each patchwork piece.

» When adjacent pieces are divided with a gray line, use the same fabric.

» Always press the seam allowances in the direction indicated by the arrows.

CONSTRUCTION STEPS

1

Make two sets

2

3

4

5

6

7

Make two sets

» When cutting your fabric, add ¼" (0.6 cm) seam allowance around each patchwork piece.

» When adjacent pieces are divided with a gray line, use the same fabric.

» Always press the seam allowances in the direction indicated by the arrows.

16 Square Eyes

The bold lines extending from the top and bottom of this block contribute to the motif's unique look. When I finished this block, I was amused to find that it reminded me of an eye, complete with eyelashes! If you plan on joining several of these blocks together, I recommend combining them horizontally with borders in between.

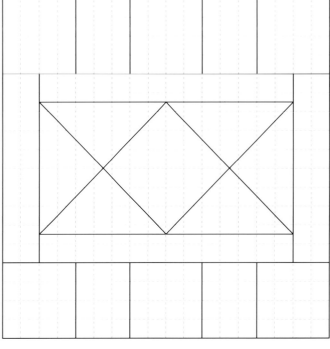

17 Royal Nine-Patch

The crown-shaped design at the center of this block lends a regal air to a pair of traditional four-patches. You can connect repeats of this motif vertically or horizontally. If you're using the blocks horizontally, I recommend rotating them 90° first for maximum impact.

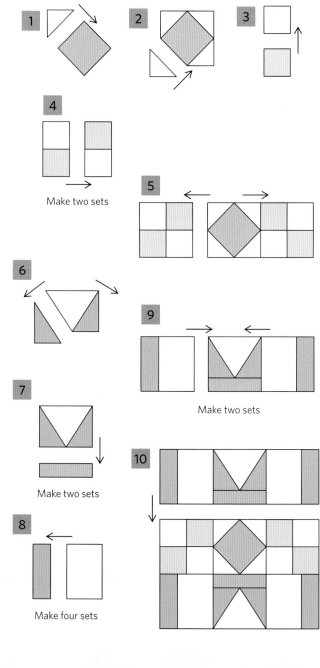

4 Make two sets

7 Make two sets

8 Make four sets

» When cutting your fabric, add ¼" (0.6 cm) seam allowance around each patchwork piece.

» When adjacent pieces are divided with a gray line, use the same fabric.

» Always press the seam allowances in the direction indicated by the arrows.

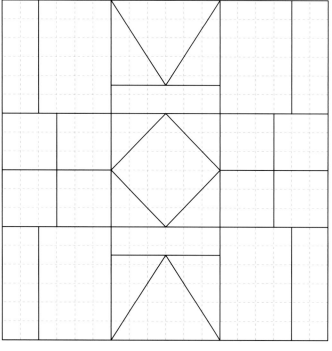

18 Square Knot

This design features a series of squares layered on top of a thin cross. The central portion of this block can be used on its own, but I chose to add a frame to make the motif stand out.

Enlarge pattern 200%

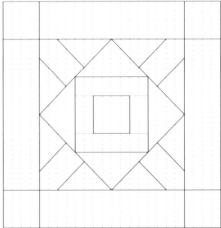

» When cutting your fabric, add ¼" (0.6 cm) seam allowance around each patchwork piece.

» When adjacent pieces are divided with a gray line, use the same fabric.

» Always press the seam allowances in the direction indicated by the arrows.

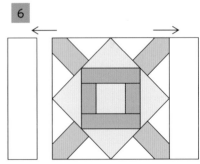

CONSTRUCTION STEPS

Make four sets

Make two sets

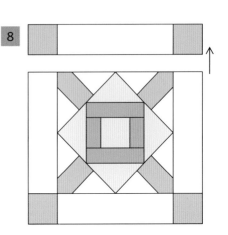

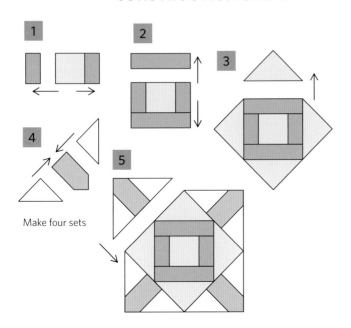

19 Bricklayer

This patchwork masterpiece is constructed by sewing ³⁄₈" (1 cm) wide pieces together, both vertically and horizontally. This process, as well as the resulting pattern, remind me of stacking bricks. Notice the pyramid-shaped designs that form on each side of the block. Keep this in mind when selecting fabric, especially if you plan on connecting multiples of this block.

» When cutting your fabric, add ¼" (0.6 cm) seam allowance around each patchwork piece.

» When adjacent pieces are divided with a gray line, use the same fabric.

» Always press the seam allowances in the direction indicated by the arrows.

CONSTRUCTION STEPS

Enlarge pattern 200%

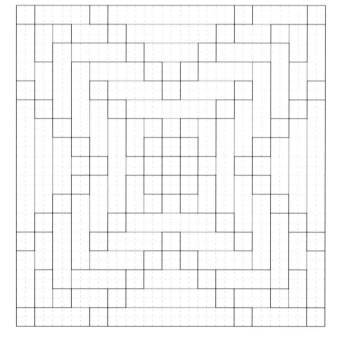

1

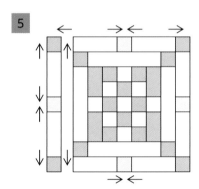

2

3

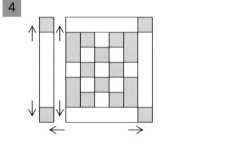

4

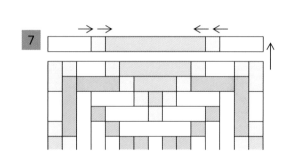

5

6

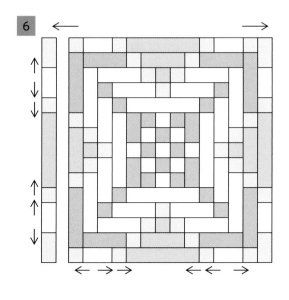

7

8

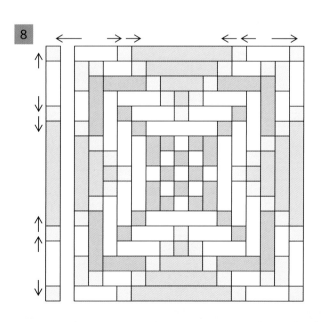

20 Crooked Pathway

Look closely and you'll see that this block is actually made up of miniature nine-patch motifs—I just changed the proportions for a new twist on an old classic. This block is featured in the Crooked Pathway Purse on page 47.

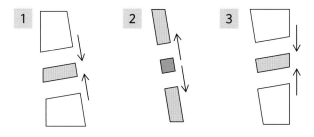

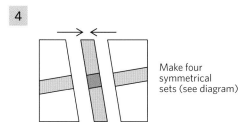

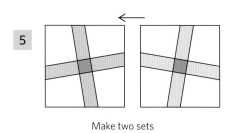

Make four symmetrical sets (see diagram)

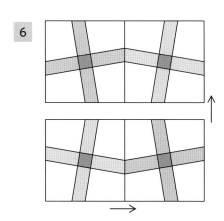

Make two sets

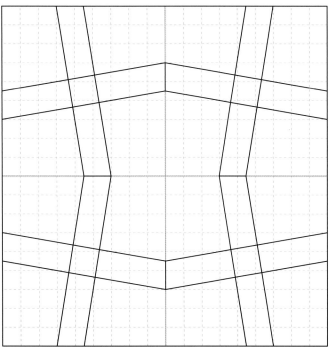

» When cutting your fabric, add ¼" (0.6 cm) seam allowance around each patchwork piece.

» When adjacent pieces are divided with a gray line, use the same fabric.

» Always press the seam allowances in the direction indicated by the arrows.

Crooked Pathway Purse

This purse is made using multiples of the **Crooked Pathway** block shown on the opposite page. When assembled, the Crooked Pathway block makes gentle vertical and horizontal zigzag lines, as well as wavy squares and crosses. Complete the purse with thin short leather handles and a few decorative beads attached to the zipper.

Instructions on page 48

MATERIALS FOR CROOKED PATHWAY PURSE

Patchwork fabric: Assorted scraps

Gusset/tab fabric: 15¾" × 17¾" (40 × 45 cm) light brown plaid

Backing: 17¾" × 19¾" (45 × 50 cm)

Batting: 17¾" × 19¾" (45 × 50 cm)

Binding: One 1⅜" × 31½" (3.5 × 80 cm) bias strip

Zipper: One 14" (35.5 cm) long zipper

Handle: 25¼" (64 cm) of ⅜" (1 cm) wide black leather tape

Cord: 6" (15 cm) of ¹⁄₃₂" (0.1 cm) diameter cord

Beads: Three ⁷⁄₁₆" (1.2 cm) diameter wooden beads

CUTTING INSTRUCTIONS

Seam allowance is not included. Add ¼" (0.6 cm) seam allowance to all piece edges.

Trace and cut out the Block #20 template on page 46 and the template on Pattern Sheet A. Cut out the pieces following the instructions listed on the templates.

Cut out the following pieces, which do not have templates, according to the measurements below:

» **Tabs (cut 2 on the bias):** 1 ³⁄₁₆" × 2 ¾" (3 × 7 cm) of gusset/tab fabric

LAYOUT DIAGRAM

TOP

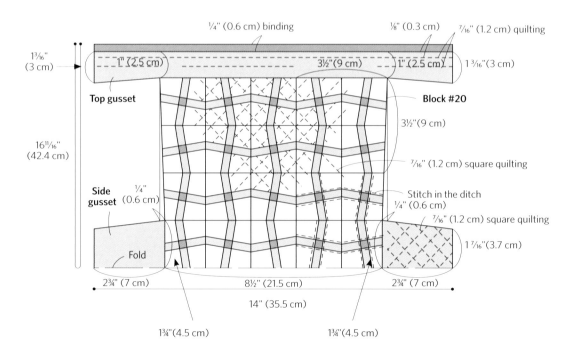

¼" (0.6 cm) binding

⅛" (0.3 cm)

⁷⁄₁₆" (1.2 cm) quilting

1³⁄₁₆"
(3 cm)

1" (2.5 cm)

3½"(9 cm)

1" (2.5 cm)

1 ³⁄₁₆"(3 cm)

Top gusset

Block #20

3½"(9 cm)

16¹¹⁄₁₆"
(42.4 cm)

⁷⁄₁₆" (1.2 cm) square quilting

**Side
gusset**

¼"
(0.6 cm)

Stitch in the ditch
¼" (0.6 cm)

⁷⁄₁₆" (1.2 cm) square quilting

1 ⁷⁄₁₆"(3.7 cm)

Fold

2¾" (7 cm)

8½" (21.5 cm)

2¾" (7 cm)

14" (35.5 cm)

1¾"(4.5 cm)

1¾"(4.5 cm)

TAB (cut 2 on bias)

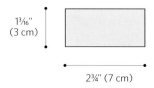

1³⁄₁₆"
(3 cm)

2¾" (7 cm)

» Stitch in the ditch around all patchwork pieces.
» Sew using ¼" (0.6 cm) seam allowance, unless
otherwise noted.

MAKE THE TOP

1. Follow the instructions on page 46 to make 12 of Block #20. To make the top, sew the blocks together in four rows of three.

2. With right sides together, sew the top gussets to the top.

3. With right sides together, sew the side gussets to the top.

4. Make a template of the top and mark the finishing lines. Cut out the top, leaving a ¼" (0.6 cm) seam allowance. Cut the batting and backing slightly larger than the assembled top. Layer the top, batting, and backing. Baste, then quilt, as shown in the Layout Diagram on page 49.

5. Bind the top gussets with bias strips.

6. Align one side of the zipper underneath one top gusset. Topstitch the binding to attach the zipper. Repeat to attach the other side of the zipper to the other top gusset. Trim excess zipper length if necessary. Slip-stitch the zipper seam allowances to the backing.

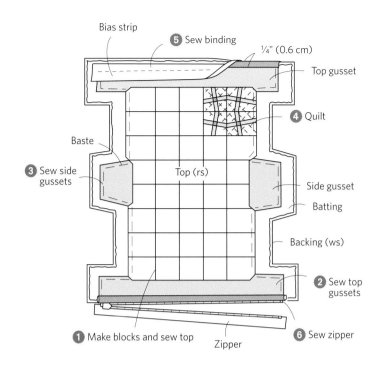

MAKE THE TABS

1. Fold each tab in half with right sides together and sew. Press the seam allowance open. Turn right side out.

2. Center the seam allowance and fold each tab in half again.

3. Baste a tab to each end of the top gussets.

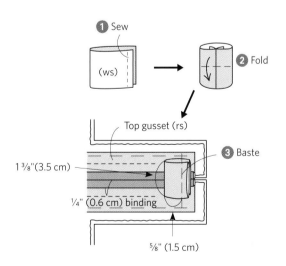

SEW THE BAG TOGETHER

1. With right sides together, sew the top and side gussets together at each end.

2. Finish the gusset seam allowances with bias strips.

3. Cut the leather tape into two equal pieces to make the handles. With the zipper open, align the ends of each handle with the right side of the bag top at an angle and baste.

4. With the zipper still open, sew the top to the gussets to close the bag at the sides.

5. Trim all seam allowances, except for the backing, to ¼" (0.6 cm).

6. On each side, wrap the backing seam allowance around the trimmed seam allowances.

7. On each side, slip-stitch the backing seam allowance to the backing.

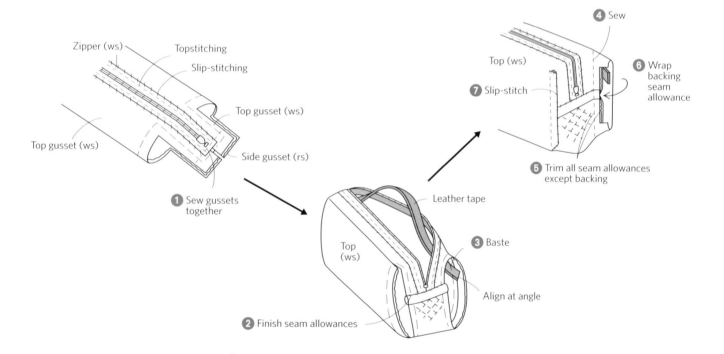

Zipper (ws)
Topstitching
Slip-stitching
Top gusset (ws)
Top gusset (ws)
Side gusset (rs)
1 Sew gussets together

4 Sew
Top (ws)
6 Wrap backing seam allowance
7 Slip-stitch
5 Trim all seam allowances except backing

Leather tape
Top (ws)
3 Baste
Align at angle
2 Finish seam allowances

MAKE THE ZIPPER CHARM

1. Fold the cord in half and tie to the zipper pull. Thread the wooden beads onto the cord, tying a knot after each bead.

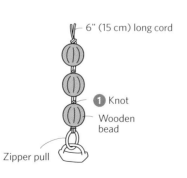

6" (15 cm) long cord
1 Knot
Wooden bead
Zipper pull

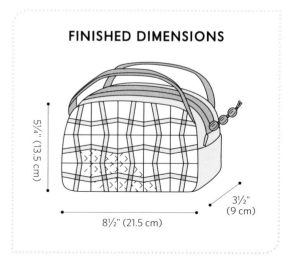

FINISHED DIMENSIONS

5¼" (13.5 cm)

3½" (9 cm)

8½" (21.5 cm)

21 Ribbon Cross

This block combines a ribbon-like cross and small triangles. Use a dark fabric to transform the small diamond in the center into the focal point of the entire block.

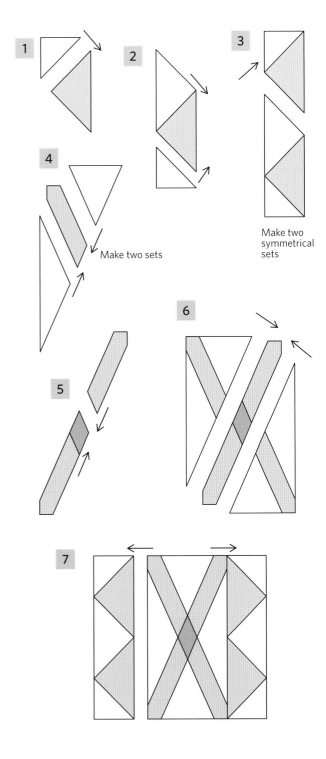

Make two sets

Make two symmetrical sets

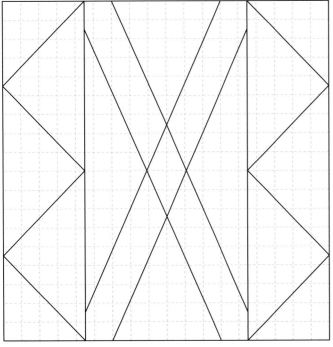

» When cutting your fabric, add ¼" (0.6 cm) seam allowance around each patchwork piece.
» When adjacent pieces are divided with a gray line, use the same fabric.
» Always press the seam allowances in the direction indicated by the arrows.

CONSTRUCTION STEPS

1

Make two sets

2

3

4

5

Make two sets

6

7

8

Make four symmetrical sets (see diagram)

9

» When cutting your fabric, add ¼" (0.6 cm) seam allowance around each patchwork piece.

» When adjacent pieces are divided with a gray line, use the same fabric.

» Always press the seam allowances in the direction indicated by the arrows.

22 Castle and Moat

In this block, a central cross motif is surrounded by a series of patchwork walls, creating the impression of a castle surrounded by a moat. The green corners overlap both the inner square and outer border, adding movement and visual interest to the block.

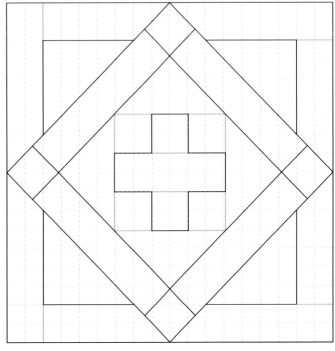

23 Crossbars

I selected a neutral background fabric for this block in order to make the darker cross motifs stand out. This design is composed of several small pieces, so it is important to keep your seams aligned for a neat finished product.

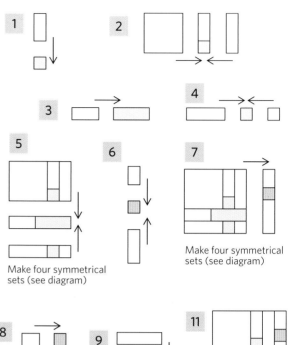

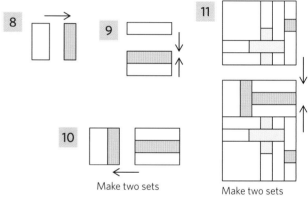

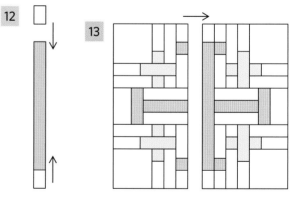

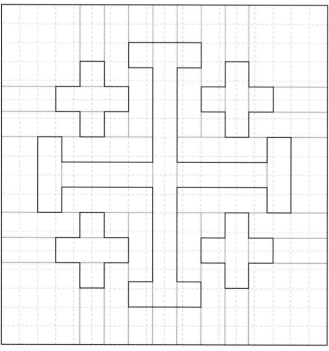

» When cutting your fabric, add ¼" (0.6 cm) seam allowance around each patchwork piece.

» When adjacent pieces are divided with a gray line, use the same fabric.

» Always press the seam allowances in the direction indicated by the arrows.

CONSTRUCTION STEPS

1

2

3

Make four sets

4

5

6

Make four symmetrical sets (see diagram)

7

Make two sets

8

» When cutting your fabric, add ¼" (0.6 cm) seam allowance around each patchwork piece.

» When adjacent pieces are divided with a gray line, use the same fabric.

» Always press the seam allowances in the direction indicated by the arrows.

24 Center Stage

This block features two powerful design elements: a shining star framed by a thick cross. The brown striped fabric used for the cross motif looks a bit like a wooden frame.

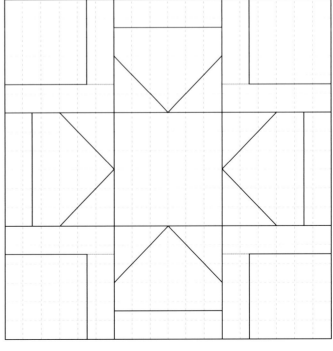

25 My Favorite Cross

Cross motifs appear frequently in my work and I enjoy playing with variations of this shape. While this might look like a simple cross block, it's actually a bit tricky to assemble. The cross is made up of many pieces that need to be aligned carefully.

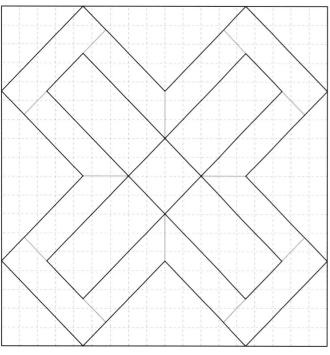

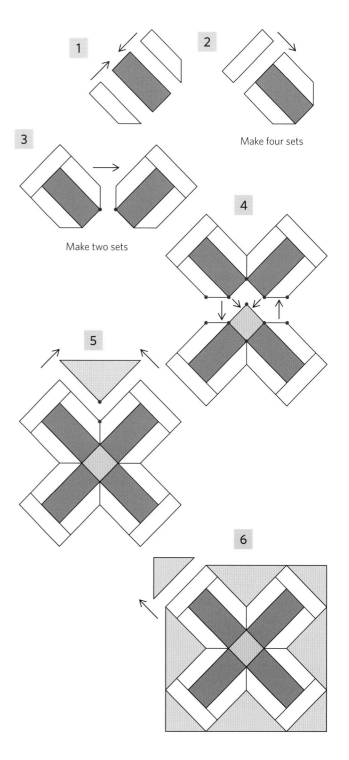

1

2

Make four sets

3

Make two sets

4

5

6

» When cutting your fabric, add ¼" (0.6 cm) seam allowance around each patchwork piece.

» When adjacent pieces are divided with a gray line, use the same fabric.

» Always press the seam allowances in the direction indicated by the arrows.

» The • marks to stop sewing at the seam allowance.

CONSTRUCTION STEPS

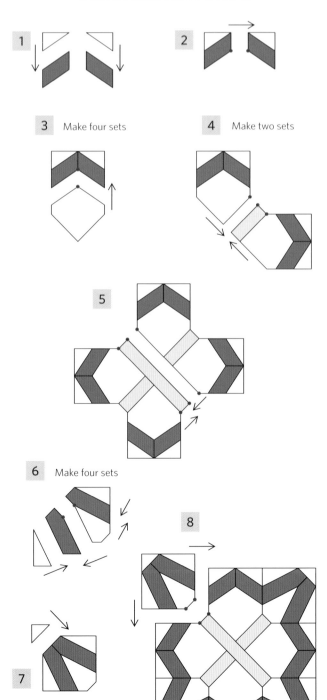

1

2

3 Make four sets

4 Make two sets

5

6 Make four sets

7

8

Zigzag Framed Cross

I used a light grid-like background fabric to create a strong contrast with the zigzag lines and center cross. This block is the star of the Framed Cross Clutch on page 58.

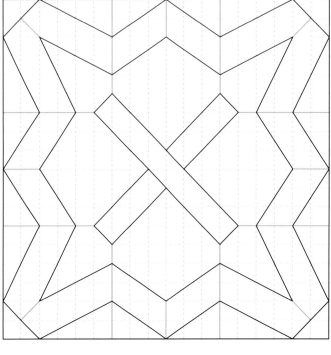

» When cutting your fabric, add ¼" (0.6 cm) seam allowance around each patchwork piece.

» When adjacent pieces are divided with a gray line, use the same fabric.

» Always press the seam allowances in the direction indicated by the arrows.

» The • marks to stop sewing at the seam allowance.

Framed Cross Clutch

This pretty little bag is trimmed with fine wale corduroy, providing a stylish touch, which makes it perfect for special occasions. I carefully positioned the three **Zigzag Framed Cross** blocks so that the designs are not hidden by the tab and are not too near the bottom or edges. As an added touch, I covered the magnetic snap and button to make the bag beautiful both inside and out.

Instructions on page 60

MATERIALS FOR FRAMED CROSS CLUTCH

Patchwork fabric: Assorted scraps

Main fabric: 19¾" × 23⅝" (50 × 60 cm) gray corduroy

Tab fabric: 4" × 6" (10 × 15 cm) brown plaid

Button covering: 2" × 2" (5 × 5 cm) green print

Backing: 17¾" × 19¾" (45 × 50 cm)

Batting: 17¾" × 19¾" (45 × 50 cm)

Binding:

    For clutch opening and tab binding: One 1⅜" × 11¾" (3.5 × 30 cm) brown corduroy bias strip

    For seam allowances: One 1³⁄₁₆" × 47¼" (3 × 120 cm) bias strip

Fusible interfacing: 2⅜" × 3⅛ (6 × 8 cm)

Piping: One 1" × 23⅝" (2.5 × 60 cm) brown corduroy bias strip

Piping cord: 23⅝" (60 cm) of ⅛" (0.3 cm) diameter cord

Button: One 1³⁄₁₆" (3 cm) diameter button

Magnetic snap: One 1³⁄₁₆" (3 cm) diameter magnetic snap set

CUTTING INSTRUCTIONS

Seam allowance is not included. Add ¼" (0.6 cm) seam allowance to all piece edges.

Trace and cut out the Block #26 template on page 57 and the templates on Pattern Sheet A. Cut out the pieces following the instructions listed on the templates.

Cut out the following pieces, which do not have templates, according to the measurements below:

» **Button covering (cut without seam allowance):** 2" (5 cm) diameter circle of button covering fabric
» **Snap coverings (cut 2 without seam allowance):** 2" (5 cm) diameter circle of main fabric

LAYOUT DIAGRAM

FRONT

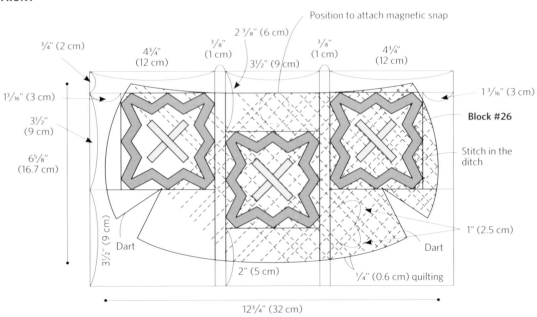

Position to attach magnetic snap

¾" (2 cm)

4¾" (12 cm)

⅜" (1 cm)

2 ⅜" (6 cm)

3½" (9 cm)

⅜" (1 cm)

4¾" (12 cm)

1 ³⁄₁₆" (3 cm)

1 ³⁄₁₆" (3 cm)

Block #26

3½" (9 cm)

Stitch in the ditch

6⅝" (16.7 cm)

3½" (9 cm) Dart

Dart

1" (2.5 cm)

2" (5 cm)

¼" (0.6 cm) quilting

12¾" (32 cm)

BACK

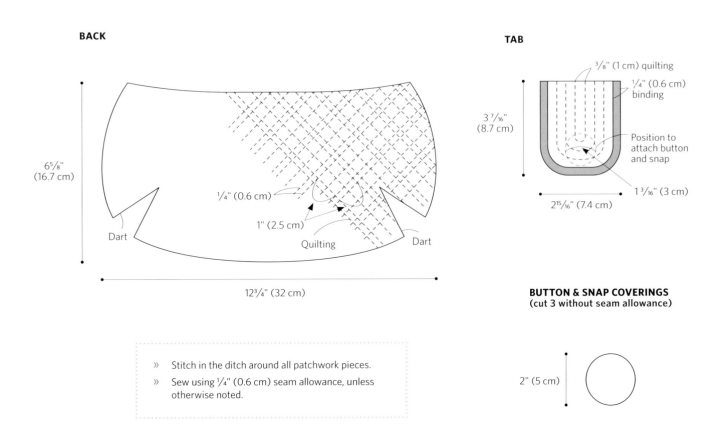

6⅝" (16.7 cm)

¼" (0.6 cm)

1" (2.5 cm)

Dart

Quilting

Dart

12¾" (32 cm)

» Stitch in the ditch around all patchwork pieces.
» Sew using ¼" (0.6 cm) seam allowance, unless otherwise noted.

TAB

⅜" (1 cm) quilting

¼" (0.6 cm) binding

3 ⁷⁄₁₆" (8.7 cm)

Position to attach button and snap

1 ³⁄₁₆" (3 cm)

2¹⁵⁄₁₆" (7.4 cm)

BUTTON & SNAP COVERINGS
(cut 3 without seam allowance)

2" (5 cm)

MAKE THE FRONT AND BACK

1. Follow the instructions on page 57 to make three of Block #26. To make the front, sew the blocks together with the front patchwork pieces.

2. Cut the batting and backing slightly larger than the assembled front. Layer the front, batting, and backing. Quilt, as shown in the Layout Diagram on page 61.

3. Make a template of the front and mark the finishing lines. Cut out the front, leaving a ⅝" (1.5 cm) seam allowance on all sides, except the opening. Do not trim the opening.

4. Sew the darts. Press dart seam allowances towards the center and slip-stitch to the backing.

5. Repeats steps 2–4 to make the back. Make sure the press the dart seam allowances in the opposite direction from the front.

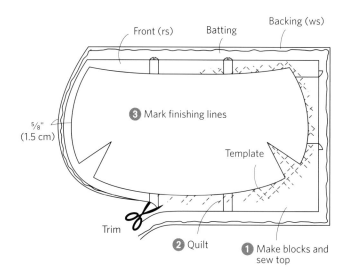

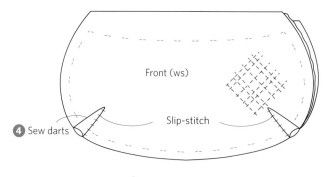

SEW THE CLUTCH TOGETHER

1. Align front and back with right sides together and sew. Start and stop sewing ¼" (0.6 cm) beyond the finishing line.

2. Sew the bias strip to the seam allowance.

3. Trim seam allowances to ¼" (0.6 cm).

4. Wrap the bias strip around the trimmed seam allowances and slip-stitch to the backing.

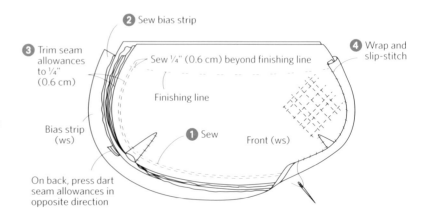

MAKE THE TAB

1. Adhere fusible interfacing to the wrong side of the tab backing.

2. Layer the tab top, batting, and tab backing. Quilt, as shown in the Layout Diagram on page 61.

3. Bind the seam allowance with a bias strip.

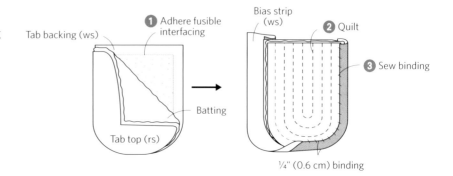

MAKE THE PIPING

1. Fold the piping bias strip in half with the piping cord sandwiched in between. Baste.

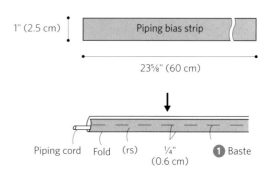

FINISH THE OPENING

① With right sides together, baste the tab to the back.

② With right sides together, pin the piping cord to the opening.

③ Slip-stitch the cord and piping ends together.

④ With right sides together, sew the bias strip to the opening along the finishing lines.

⑤ Trim the seam allowances to ¼" (0.6 cm).

⑥ Wrap the bias strip around the trimmed seam allowances and slip-stitch to the backing.

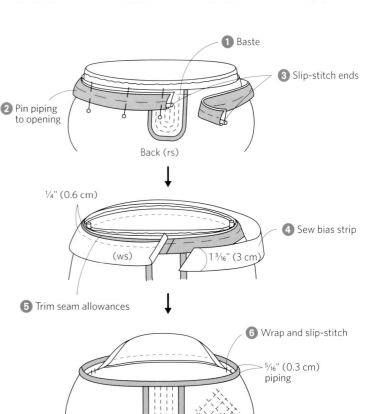

① Baste

③ Slip-stitch ends

② Pin piping to opening

Back (rs)

¼" (0.6 cm)

(ws)

④ Sew bias strip

1 ³⁄₁₆" (3 cm)

⑤ Trim seam allowances

⑥ Wrap and slip-stitch

⁵⁄₁₆" (0.3 cm) piping

ADD THE BUTTON AND SNAP

① Running stitch around the circular fabric scrap, then pull thread tails to gather around button. Repeat for both components of the magnetic snap.

② Slip-stitch the wrapped button to the tab top.

③ Slip-stitch one magnetic snap component to the tab backing and one to the clutch front.

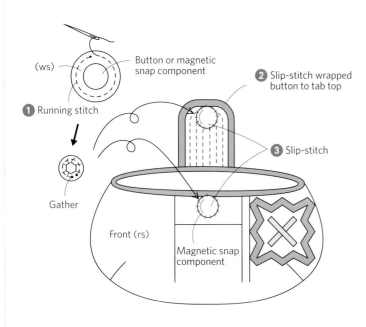

(ws)

Button or magnetic snap component

① Running stitch

Gather

② Slip-stitch wrapped button to tab top

③ Slip-stitch

Front (rs)

Magnetic snap component

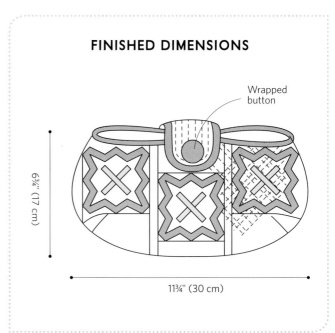

FINISHED DIMENSIONS

Wrapped button

6¾" (17 cm)

11¾" (30 cm)

CONSTRUCTION STEPS

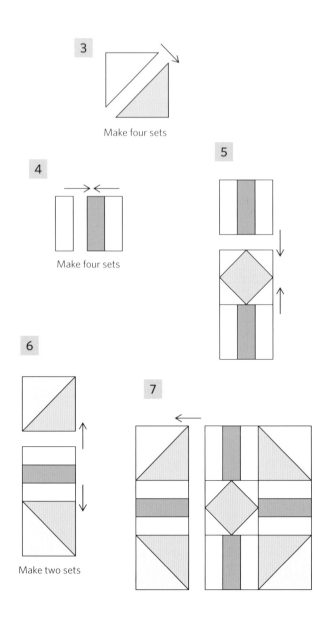

1

2

3

Make four sets

4

Make four sets

5

6

7

Make two sets

27

Footbridge

This block showcases the versatility of fabrics featuring directional patterns. In this block, dark brown fabric is used for a large central cross motif, while the lighter striped corner pieces form a subtle cross in the background.

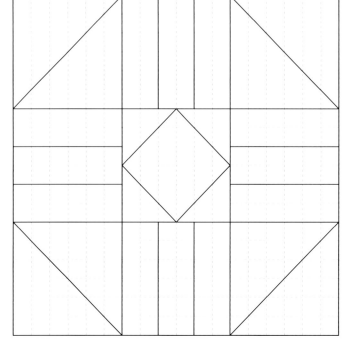

» When cutting your fabric, add ¼" (0.6 cm) seam allowance around each patchwork piece.

» When adjacent pieces are divided with a gray line, use the same fabric.

» Always press the seam allowances in the direction indicated by the arrows.

28 Double Cross

With this block, I continued to experiment with directional patterns in an effort to create a three-dimensional effect. When you connect repeats of this motif, the thick striped crosses combine to make a powerful impression.

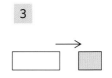

1

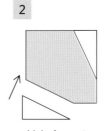

2

Make four sets

3

Make four sets

4

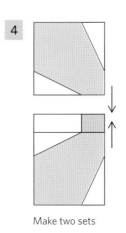

5

Make two sets

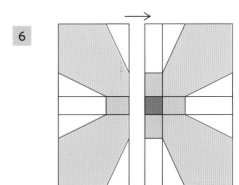

6

- » When cutting your fabric, add ¼" (0.6 cm) seam allowance around each patchwork piece.
- » When adjacent pieces are divided with a gray line, use the same fabric.
- » Always press the seam allowances in the direction indicated by the arrows.

CONSTRUCTION STEPS

1

2

3

4

Make four sets

5 Make two sets

6

7

29 Spinning Jack

Can you count the number of crosses hidden within this block? Thin rectangles intersect a large double X motif to form a series of six crosses. I appliquéd a small square at the center to balance out the design of this block, which was inspired by the old-fashioned playground game.

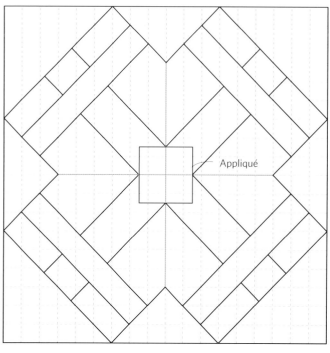

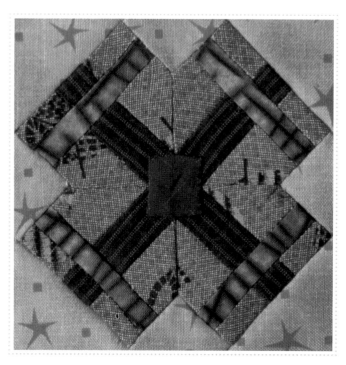

Appliqué

8

Appliqué

» When cutting your fabric, add ¼" (0.6 cm) seam allowance around each patchwork piece.

» When adjacent pieces are divided with a gray line, use the same fabric.

» Always press the seam allowances in the direction indicated by the arrows.

» The • marks to stop sewing at the seam allowance.

30 Near and Far

This is another block with the appearance of dimensional depth. A large X crosses over a smaller square, creating the illusion that it is receding into space. The depth in this block is further emphasized by your choice of background fabric. I used a woven plaid with subtle color gradation.

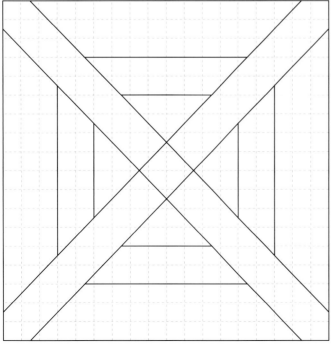

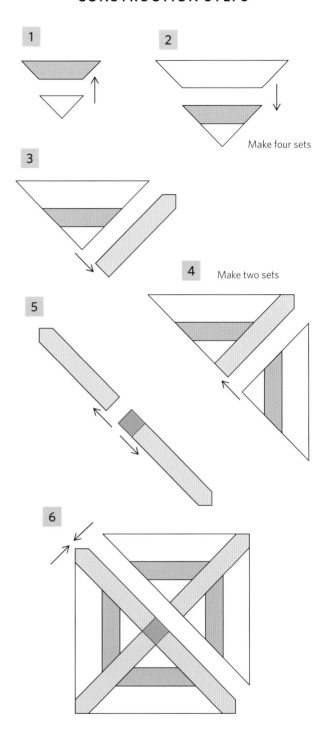

1

2

Make four sets

3

4   Make two sets

5

6

» When cutting your fabric, add ¼" (0.6 cm) seam allowance around each patchwork piece.
» When adjacent pieces are divided with a gray line, use the same fabric.
» Always press the seam allowances in the direction indicated by the arrows.

CONSTRUCTION STEPS

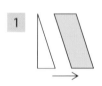

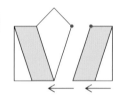

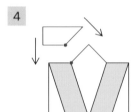

3

4

5

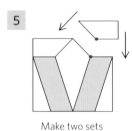

Make two sets

6

7   Repeat steps 1-6 for right side

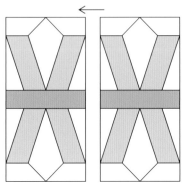

» When cutting your fabric, add ¼" (0.6 cm) seam allowance around each patchwork piece.

» When adjacent pieces are divided with a gray line, use the same fabric.

» Always press the seam allowances in the direction indicated by the arrows.

» The • marks to stop sewing at the seam allowance.

31 Twins

These side-by-side X motifs appear to be tied together in the center with a ribbon-like rectangle. If you use multiples of this block, align them horizontally so the rectangles connect to form a straight line.

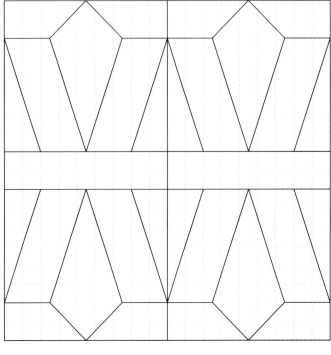

32 Dancer on a Ball

This block features the classic Drunkard's Path motif as its focal point. Adding a frame made out of coordinating fabrics breathes new life into an old favorite.

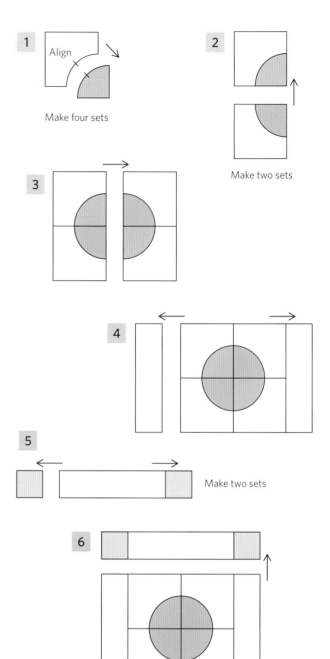

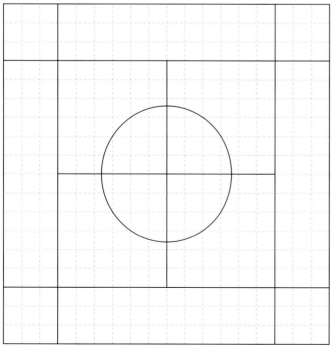

» When cutting your fabric, add ¼" (0.6 cm) seam allowance around each patchwork piece.

» When adjacent pieces are divided with a gray line, use the same fabric.

» Always press the seam allowances in the direction indicated by the arrows.

CONSTRUCTION STEPS

1

2

Make two sets

3

4

5

Make four sets

6

7

33 Waterwheel

Several different shapes work together in harmony to power this geometric block design. A hollow circle, diamond blades, and a thin central cross combine to form a waterwheel motif. I recommend using a contrasting accent fabric for the diamonds to make them pop.

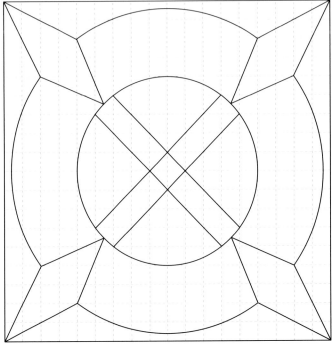

» When cutting your fabric, add ¼" (0.6 cm) seam allowance around each patchwork piece.

» When adjacent pieces are divided with a gray line, use the same fabric.

» Always press the seam allowances in the direction indicated by the arrows.

» The • marks to stop sewing at the seam allowance.

34 Thirteen

When I first started designing this block, I set out to replicate my grandmother's favorite fan. In the end, I decided to turn one of the thin strips into a cross, forming the Roman numeral thirteen. It's funny how a design can take on a totally new direction midway through the creative process. You can make this block using the patchwork technique illustrated in the construction steps, or create the thin strips using appliqué.

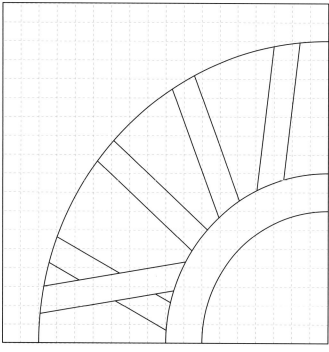

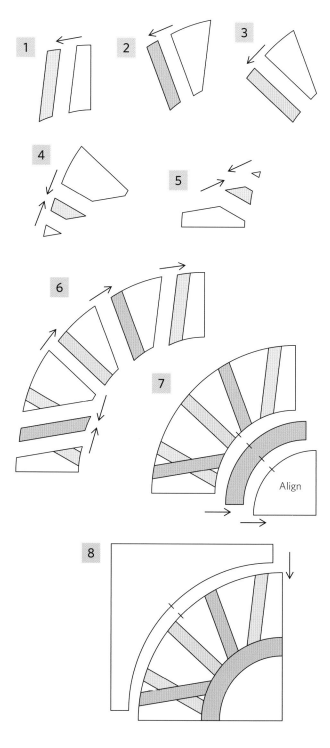

» When cutting your fabric, add ¼" (0.6 cm) seam allowance around each patchwork piece.
» When adjacent pieces are divided with a gray line, use the same fabric.
» Always press the seam allowances in the direction indicated by the arrows.

35 Sundial

Enlarge pattern 200%

The combination of the light background fabric and boldly curved border make the sun motif appear as if it is bursting out of this eye-catching block. This design contains several sharp points and shallow curves, so it is essential to sew the pieces together carefully. Don't forget to use a lot of pins!

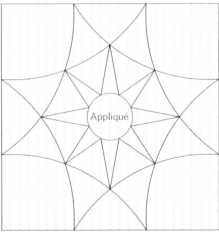

» When cutting your fabric, add 1/4" (0.6 cm) seam allowance around each patchwork piece.
» When adjacent pieces are divided with a gray line, use the same fabric.
» Always press the seam allowances in the direction indicated by the arrows.

7

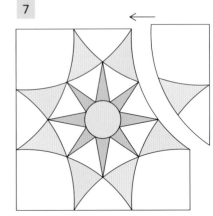

CONSTRUCTION STEPS

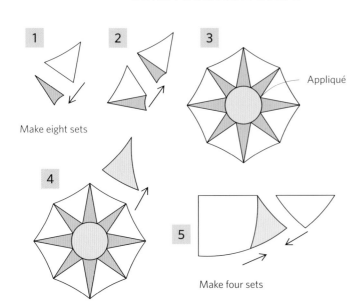

1

2

3

Appliqué

Make eight sets

4

6

5

Make four sets

36 Puzzle Ring

This block is composed of two of the most basic shapes—a circle and a rectangle—yet, the manner in which these motifs are combined creates a fascinating geometric design. This puzzling block is constructed from the inside out, allowing the rectangle to weave in and out of the circle. This effect is amplified when several repeats are connected.

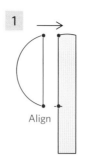

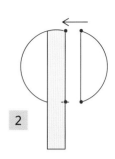

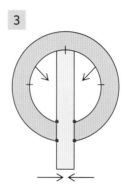

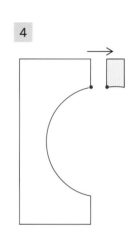

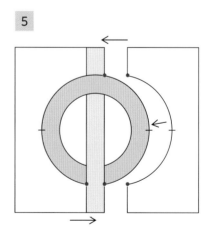

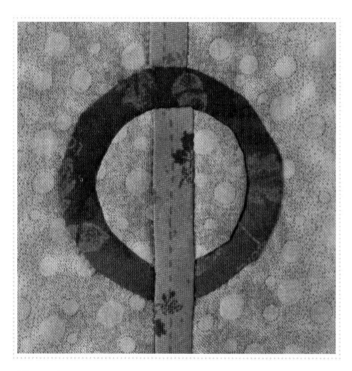

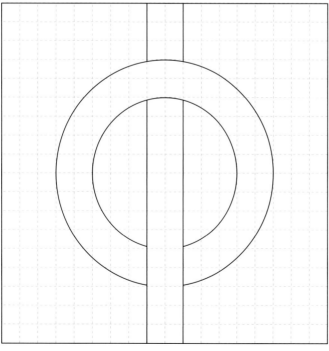

» When cutting your fabric, add ¼" (0.6 cm) seam allowance around each patchwork piece.

» When adjacent pieces are divided with a gray line, use the same fabric.

» Always press the seam allowances in the direction indicated by the arrows.

» The • marks to stop sewing at the seam allowance.

CONSTRUCTION STEPS

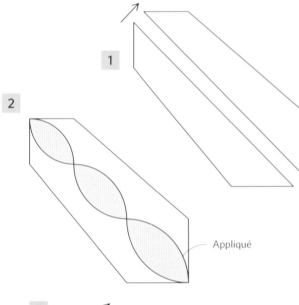

1

2

Appliqué

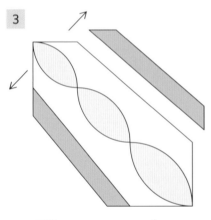

3

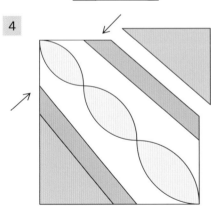

4

» When cutting your fabric, add ¼" (0.6 cm) seam allowance around each patchwork piece.

» When adjacent pieces are divided with a gray line, use the same fabric.

» Always press the seam allowances in the direction indicated by the arrows.

37 Crescendo

In this block, the diagonal stripes are made with patchwork, while the curved central motif is appliquéd. The appliqué grows wider at the bottom, making the helix appear as if it is moving.

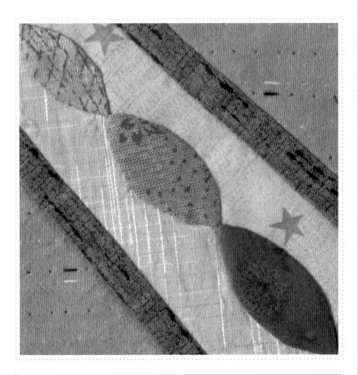

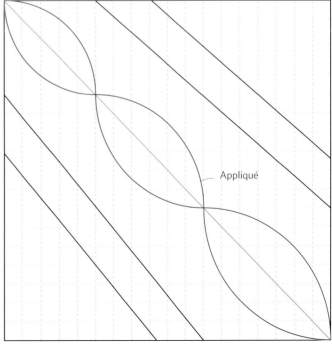

Appliqué

38 Shake Hands

This design works best when several blocks are connected. When you position all of the blocks in the same direction, thin lines form throughout the work. For a fun variation, alternate every other block by rotating 90°.

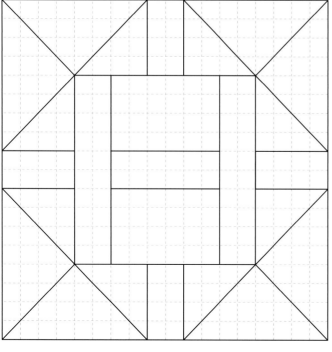

CONSTRUCTION STEPS

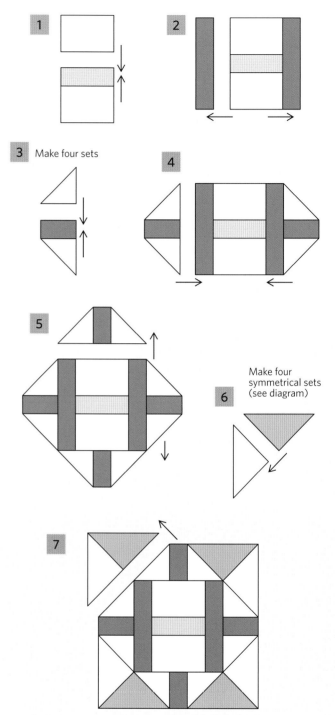

1

2

3 Make four sets

4

5

6 Make four symmetrical sets (see diagram)

7

» When cutting your fabric, add ¼" (0.6 cm) seam allowance around each patchwork piece.

» When adjacent pieces are divided with a gray line, use the same fabric.

» Always press the seam allowances in the direction indicated by the arrows.

39 Spinning Capsules

A hexagon motif is set into each quadrant of this geometric block. The hexagons alternate vertically and horizontally, making them appear as if they are spinning. Notice the large diamond outline that forms at the center of the block—it looks as if it has been stamped into the fabric.

Enlarge pattern 200%

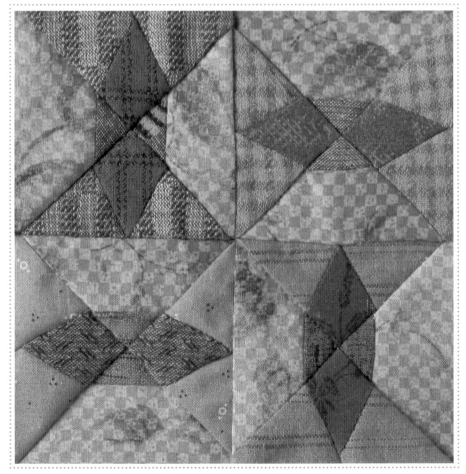

» When cutting your fabric, add ¼" (0.6 cm) seam allowance around each patchwork piece.
» When adjacent pieces are divided with a gray line, use the same fabric.
» Always press the seam allowances in the direction indicated by the arrows.

CONSTRUCTION STEPS

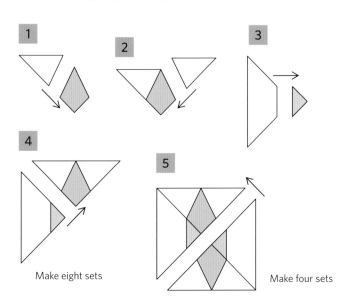

Make eight sets

Make four sets

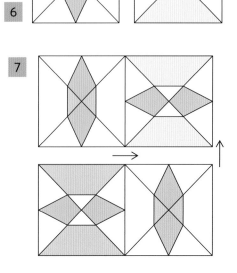

40 Little Wedges

The blue wedges and black frame featured in this design are actually made from the same template, but I used different fabrics to make the two elements distinct. I love the way the wedges appear as if they are sitting on top of the frame.

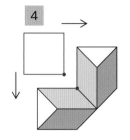

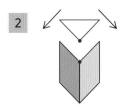

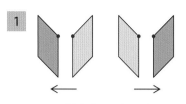

Make four sets each

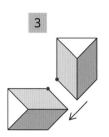

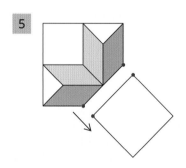

Make four sets

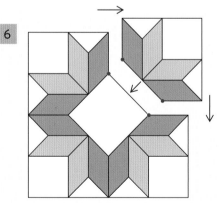

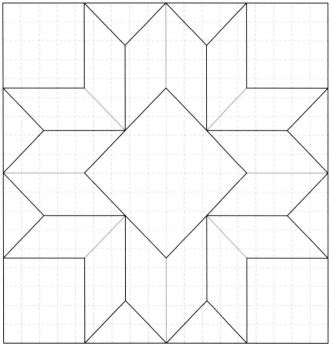

» When cutting your fabric, add ¼" (0.6 cm) seam allowance around each patchwork piece.

» When adjacent pieces are divided with a gray line, use the same fabric.

» Always press the seam allowances in the direction indicated by the arrows.

» The • marks to stop sewing at the seam allowance.

CONSTRUCTION STEPS

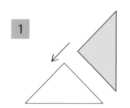

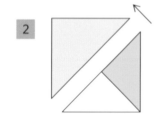

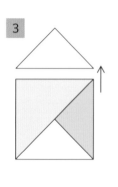

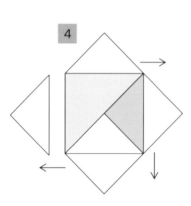

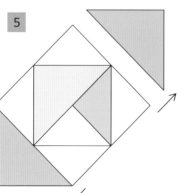

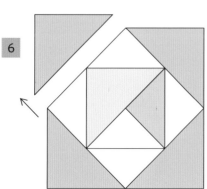

41 Triangle Collection

This simple block is made using three kinds of triangles. Add stability to its design by using a darker fabric for the two smaller triangle pieces in the center of the block. Try using the block on a 45° angle or embellishing the seams with embroidery.

» When cutting your fabric, add ¼" (0.6 cm) seam allowance around each patchwork piece.

» When adjacent pieces are divided with a gray line, use the same fabric.

» Always press the seam allowances in the direction indicated by the arrows.

42 Confetti

The miniature squares sprinkled throughout this motif appear as if they are floating in midair. If you plan on joining multiples of this motif together, I recommend adding a border made of background fabric between each block, as seen in the Confetti Purse on the opposite page. Use a bright accent color for the central square of each block to make this design come alive.

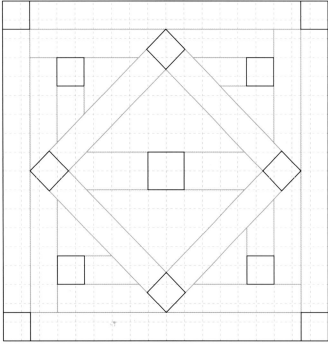

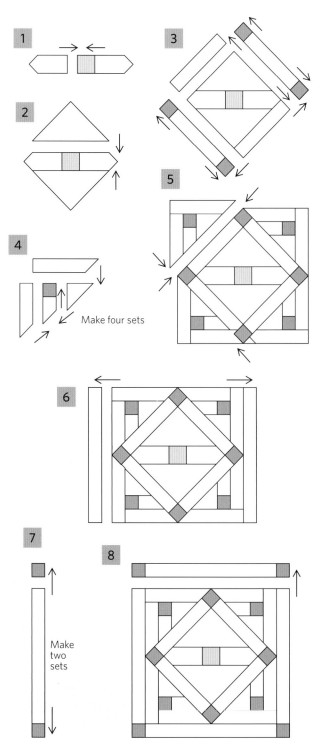

» When cutting your fabric, add ¼" (0.6 cm) seam allowance around each patchwork piece.

» When adjacent pieces are divided with a gray line, use the same fabric.

» Always press the seam allowances in the direction indicated by the arrows.

Confetti Purse

With its short handles and rectangular silhouette, this bag reminds me of a briefcase. When selecting fabric for this project, I chose materials with a similar, dark tone for the gusset, binding, and **Confetti** block backgrounds in order to make the small squares appear as if they are floating in midair...just like real confetti!

Instructions on page 82

MATERIALS FOR CONFETTI PURSE

Patchwork fabric: Assorted scraps

Main fabric: 19¾" × 43¼" (50 × 110 cm) black print

Gusset/tab fabric: 11¾" × 27½" (30 × 70 cm) black woven print

Backing: 25½" × 33½" (65 × 85 cm)

Batting: 25½" × 33½" (65 × 85 cm)

Binding:

> **For top gusset:** One 1⅜" × 39⅜" (3.5 × 100 cm) black plaid bias strip

> **For seam allowances:** One 1⅜" × 90 9/16" (3.5 × 230 cm) bias strip

Fusible interfacing: 7⅞" × 27½" (20 × 70 cm)

Zipper: One 18" (45.5 cm) long zipper

Handles: One set of 6¾" (17 cm) long leather handles

Cord: 15¾" (40 cm) of ⅛" (0.3 cm) diameter cord and 4" (10 cm) of 1/32" (0.1 cm) diameter cord

Beads: One 5/16" (0.8 cm) diameter bead and one 1³/16" (3 cm) diameter wooden bead

CUTTING INSTRUCTIONS

Seam allowance is not included. Add ¼" (0.6 cm) seam allowance to all piece edges.

Trace and cut out the Block #42 template on page 80 and the templates on Pattern Sheet B. Cut out the pieces following the instructions listed on the templates.

Cut out the following pieces, which do not have templates, according to the measurements below:

> » **Top gusset (cut 2):** 1³/16" × 17 ¼" (3 × 44 cm) of gusset/tab fabric
> » **Top gusset interfacing (cut 2 without seam allowance):** 1³/16" × 17 ¼" (3 × 44 cm) of fusible interfacing
> » **Bottom gusset:** 2 ⅜" × 25 ¼" (6 × 64 cm) of gusset/tab fabric
> » **Bottom gusset interfacing (cut without seam allowance):** 2 ⅜" × 25 ¼" (6 × 64 cm) of fusible interfacing

LAYOUT DIAGRAM

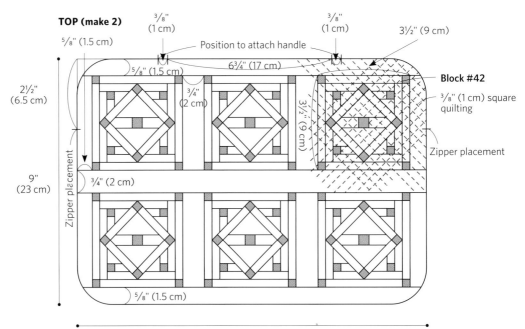

TOP GUSSET

¼" (0.6 cm)
binding

⁷⁄₁₆" (1.2 cm)
quilting

1 ³⁄₁₆" (3 cm)

2 ³⁄₈" (6 cm)

1 ³⁄₁₆" (3 cm)

17¼" (44 cm)

BOTTOM GUSSET

⁷⁄₁₆" (1.2 cm)
quilting

2 ³⁄₈"
(6 cm)

25¼" (64 cm)

TAB (cut 4)

³⁄₄"
(2 cm)

1 ⁷⁄₁₆"
(3.7 cm)

» Stitch in the ditch around all patchwork pieces.

» Sew using ¼" (0.6 cm) seam allowance, unless otherwise noted.

MAKE THE TOPS

1. Follow the instructions on page 80 to make 12 of Block #42. To make each top, sew six blocks together with the patchwork pieces.

2. Cut the battings and backings slightly larger than the assembled tops. Layer each top, batting, and backing. Quilt, as shown in the Layout Diagram on page 82.

3. Make a template of the top. Mark the finishing lines and trim into shape, leaving a large seam allowance.

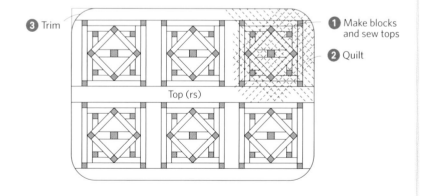

3 Trim

Top (rs)

1 Make blocks and sew tops

2 Quilt

MAKE THE TOP GUSSET

1. Cut the batting and backing slightly larger than the top gusset. Adhere the fusible interfacing to the wrong side of the top gusset backing.

2. Layer the top gusset, batting, and backing. Baste, then quilt, as shown in the Layout Diagram on page 83.

3. Bind one long edge of the top gusset using the bias strip.

4. Repeat steps 1-3 to make another top gusset.

5. Align the two top gussets and baste together around the outer edges.

6. Sew the zipper to the top gussets along each side.

7. Slip-stitch the zipper seam allowances to the top gusset backing, trimming excess zipper length if necessary.

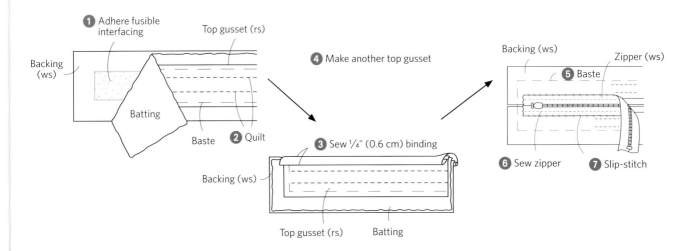

MAKE THE TAB

1. Layer two tab pieces and batting with right sides together.
   Sew, leaving the bottom open. Trim the excess seam allowances and turn right side out.

2. Topstitch using a ¼" (0.6 cm) seam allowance.

3. Repeat steps 1-2 to make another tab.

4. Align each tab with a short edge of the top gusset and baste.

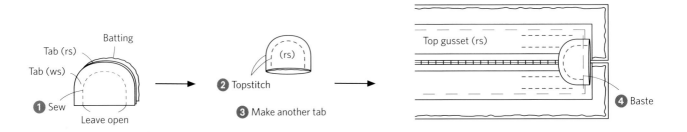

MAKE THE BOTTOM GUSSET

1 Cut the batting and backing slightly larger than the bottom gusset. Adhere fusible interfacing to the wrong side of the backing.

2 Layer the bottom gusset, batting, and backing. Baste, then quilt, as shown in the Layout Diagram on page 83.

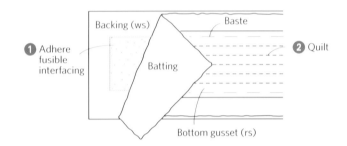

SEW THE BAG TOGETHER

1 Align the top and bottom gussets with right sides together. Sew together along the short edges to make a loop. Make sure to start and stop sewing ¼" (0.6 cm) beyond the finishing line.

2 Trim all seam allowances, except for the bottom gusset backing, to ¼" (0.6 cm).

3 On each side, wrap the bottom gusset backing seam allowance around the trimmed seam allowances and slip-stitch.

4 With right sides together, sew the assembled gusset to the tops, leaving ⅜" (1 cm) openings at the positions to attach the handles, as shown in the Layout Diagram on page 82.

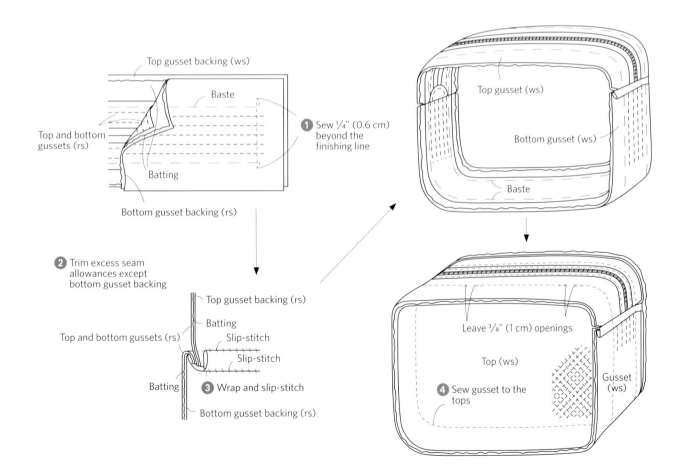

ATTACH THE HANDLES

1 Thread a 4" (10 cm) long piece of ⅛" (0.3 cm) diameter cord through each handle and fold the cord in half.

2 Insert each cord through an opening in the bag.

3 Sew to firmly attach the cords. Trim excess cord length if necessary.

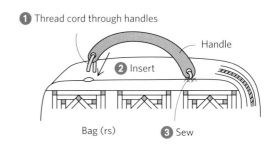

1 Thread cord through handles

Handle

2 Insert

Bag (rs)

3 Sew

FINISH THE SEAM ALLOWANCES

1 Sew the bias strip to the seam allowances. Overlap the short ends of the bias strip and sew together.

2 Trim seam allowances.

3 Wrap the bias strip around the trimmed seam allowances and slip-stitch to the backing.

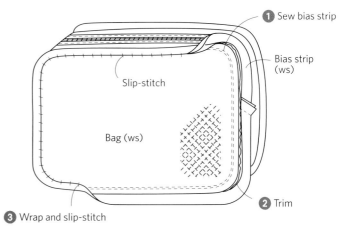

1 Sew bias strip

Bias strip (ws)

Slip-stitch

Bag (ws)

2 Trim

3 Wrap and slip-stitch

MAKE THE ZIPPER CHARM

1 Thread the beads onto the ¹⁄₃₂" (0.1 cm) diameter cord. Tie the cord to the zipper pull. Add a dab of glue to secure the knot.

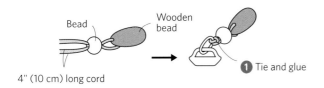

Bead

Wooden bead

4" (10 cm) long cord

1 Tie and glue

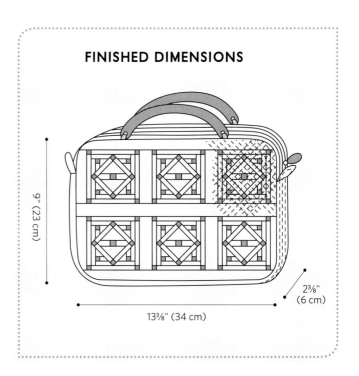

FINISHED DIMENSIONS

9" (23 cm)

13⅜" (34 cm)

2⅜" (6 cm)

CONSTRUCTION STEPS

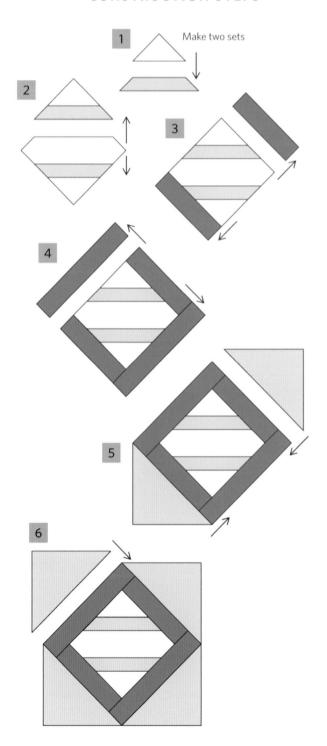

1 Make two sets

2

3

4

5

6

43 Diamond Window

This is a simple, yet versatile block design. Rotate 90° to change the horizontal lines inside the window to vertical ones. You can also turn the pattern on a 45° angle so the parallel lines are slanted. When it comes to this block, the possibilities are endless!

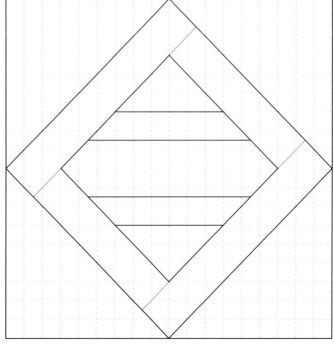

» When cutting your fabric, add ¼" (0.6 cm) seam allowance around each patchwork piece.

» When adjacent pieces are divided with a gray line, use the same fabric.

» Always press the seam allowances in the direction indicated by the arrows.

44 Up the Stairs

When I designed this block, my goal was to create a motif that was strong enough to be used on its own, but would also form an interesting secondary pattern when repeated. The stunning results are visible in the Sunday Stroll Purse pictured on the opposite page.

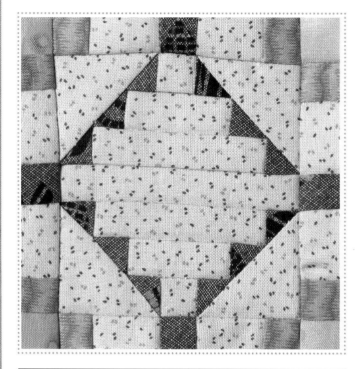

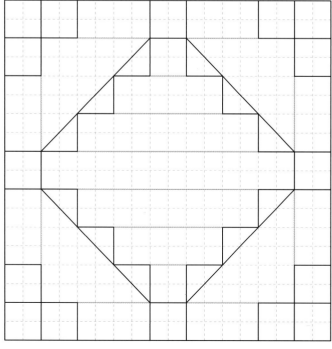

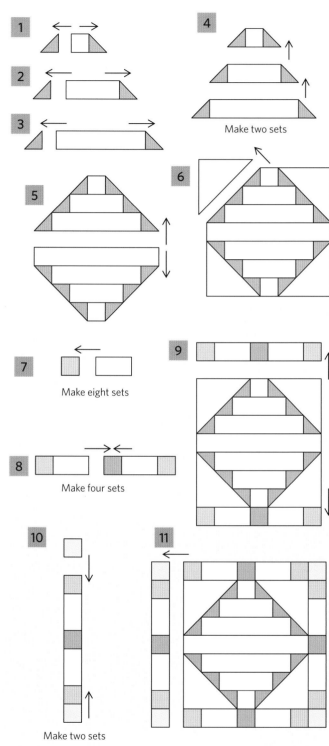

Make two sets

Make eight sets

Make four sets

Make two sets

» When cutting your fabric, add ¼" (0.6 cm) seam allowance around each patchwork piece.

» When adjacent pieces are divided with a gray line, use the same fabric.

» Always press the seam allowances in the direction indicated by the arrows.

Sunday Stroll Purse

This project is a perfect example of that mysterious quilting magic which can produce beautiful designs just by repeating a single motif. When four **Up the Stairs** blocks are connected, a striking diamond emerges at their center.

Instructions on page 90

MATERIALS FOR SUNDAY STROLL PURSE

Patchwork fabric: Assorted scraps

Main fabric: 11¾" × 11¾" (30 × 30 cm) beige print

Back fabric: 9¾" × 9¾" (25 × 25 cm) green leaf print

Gusset fabric: 6" × 23⅝" (15 × 60 cm) tan plaid

Backing: 15¾" × 23⅝" (40 × 60 cm)

Batting: 15¾" × 23⅝" (40 × 60 cm)

Binding: One 1" × 21¾" (2.5 × 55 cm) bias strip

Fusible interfacing: 4" × 23⅝" (10 × 60 cm)

Nylon web tape: 19¾" (50 cm) of ¾" (2 cm) wide beige nylon web tape

Suede tape: 19¾" (50 cm) of ⅝" (1.5 cm) wide beige suede tape

CUTTING INSTRUCTIONS

Seam allowance is not included. Add ¼" (0.6 cm) seam allowance to all piece edges.

Trace and cut out the Block #44 template on page 88 and the template on Pattern Sheet B. Cut out the pieces following the instructions listed on the templates.

Cut out the following pieces, which do not have templates, according to the measurements below:

» **Gusset:** 3⅛" × 21¾" (8 × 55 cm) of gusset fabric (trim to taper ends as shown in Layout Diagram on page 91)

» **Gusset interfacing (cut without seam allowance):** 3⅛" × 21¾" (8 × 55 cm) of gusset fabric (trim to taper ends as shown in Layout Diagram on page 91)

LAYOUT DIAGRAM

FRONT

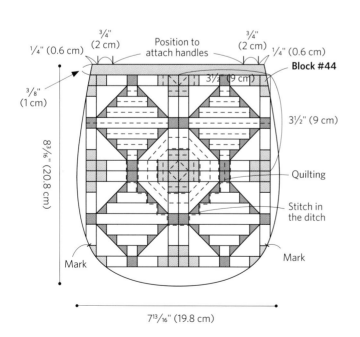

BACK

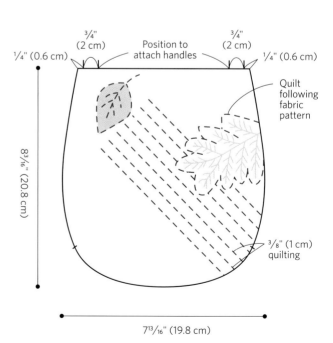

GUSSET

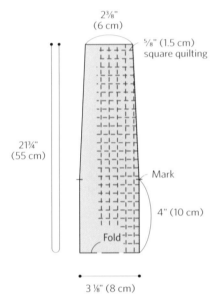

2⅜"
(6 cm)

⅝" (1.5 cm)
square quilting

21¾"
(55 cm)

Mark

4" (10 cm)

Fold

3 ⅛" (8 cm)

HANDLES (make 2)

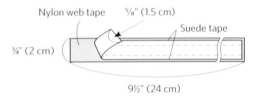

Nylon web tape   ⅝" (1.5 cm)

Suede tape

¾" (2 cm)

9½" (24 cm)

» Stitch in the ditch around all patchwork pieces.
» Sew using ¼" (0.6 cm) seam allowance, unless otherwise noted.

MAKE THE FRONT

1 Follow the instructions on page 88 to make four of Block #44. To make the front, sew four blocks together with the patchwork pieces.

2 Cut the batting and backing slightly larger than the assembled front. Layer the front, batting, and backing. Quilt, as shown in the Layout Diagram on page 90.

3 Make a template of the front. Mark the finishing lines and trim into shape, leaving a large seam allowance.

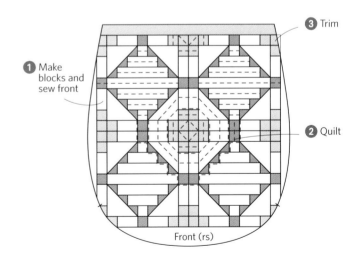

3 Trim

1 Make blocks and sew front

2 Quilt

Front (rs)

MAKE THE BACK

① Cut the batting and backing slightly larger than the back. Layer the back, batting, and backing. Quilt, as shown in the Layout Diagram on page 90.

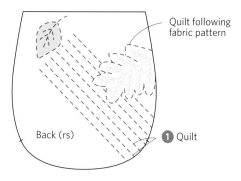

Quilt following fabric pattern

Back (rs)

① Quilt

MAKE THE GUSSET

① Cut the batting and backing slightly larger than the gusset. Adhere fusible interfacing to the wrong side of the backing.

② Layer the gusset, batting, and backing. Baste, then quilt, as shown in the Layout Diagram on page 91.

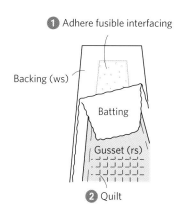

① Adhere fusible interfacing

Backing (ws)

Batting

Gusset (rs)

② Quilt

SEW THE BAG TOGETHER

① With right sides together, align the gusset with the front and back at marks. Sew the gusset to the front and back.

② Trim all seam allowances, except for the gusset backing, to ¼" (0.6 cm).

③ On each side, wrap the gusset backing seam allowances around the trimmed seam allowances and slip-stitch.

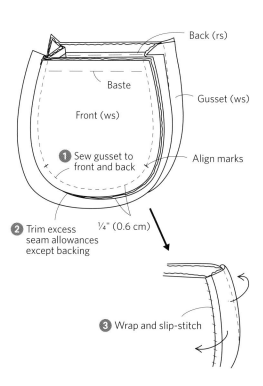

Back (rs)

Baste

Gusset (ws)

Front (ws)

① Sew gusset to front and back

Align marks

② Trim excess seam allowances except backing

¼" (0.6 cm)

③ Wrap and slip-stitch

MAKE THE HANDLES

1 Cut the nylon web tape and suede tape as shown in the Layout Diagram on page 91. For each handle, layer the suede tape on top of the nylon web tape and sew together along the long edges.

2 Baste the handles to the bag.

3 With right sides together, sew the bias strip to the bag opening. Overlap the short ends of the bias strip and sew together.

4 Trim the seam allowances to ¼" (0.6 cm).

5 Fold the bias strip to the inside of the bag. Wrap the bias strip around the trimmed seam allowances and slip-stitch to the backing.

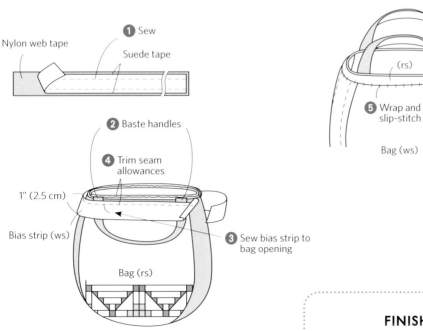

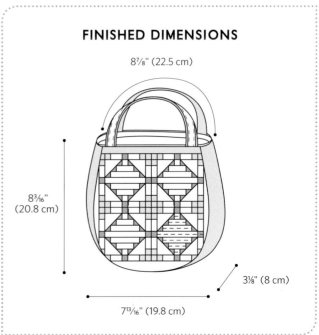

45 Diamond Four-Patch

This simple diamond four-patch block is quick and easy to sew. Because this block possesses a minimalist design, I was free to experiment with color and pattern. The combination of plaid and striped fabrics in contrasting hues adds a playful air to this motif, which is used in the whimsical Pyramid Zipper Bag on the opposite page.

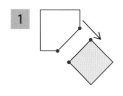

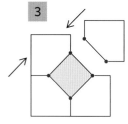

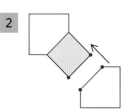

Make four sets

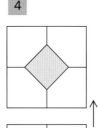

Make two sets

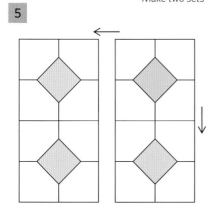

» When cutting your fabric, add ¼" (0.6 cm) seam allowance around each patchwork piece.

» When adjacent pieces are divided with a gray line, use the same fabric.

» Always press the seam allowances in the direction indicated by the arrows.

» The • marks to stop sewing at the seam allowance.

Pyramid Zipper Bag

This truly unique bag features a triangular pyramid shape, angled zipper, and a single looped handle. For a special touch, I used a cube-shaped zipper charm, which resembles the squares in the **Diamond Four-Patch** blocks featured in this design.

Instructions on page 96

MATERIALS FOR PYRAMID ZIPPER BAG

Patchwork fabric: Assorted scraps

Bottom fabric: 7⅞" × 9¾" (20 × 25 cm) brown corduroy

Bottom foundation fabric: 7⅞" × 9¾" (20 × 25 cm)

Handle fabric: 4" × 13¾" (10 × 35 cm) each brown tweed and dark brown print bias strips

Backing: 23⅝" × 27½" (60 × 70 cm)

Batting: 23⅝" × 27½" (60 × 70 cm)

Heavyweight fusible interfacing: 9¾" × 11¾" (25 × 30 cm)

Zipper: One 7" (18 cm) long zipper

Cord: 2⅜" (6 cm) of 1/32" (0.1 cm) diameter cord

Bead: One square wooden bead

CUTTING INSTRUCTIONS

Seam allowance is not included. Add ¼" (0.6 cm) seam allowance to all piece edges.

Trace and cut out the Block #45 template on page 94 and the templates on Pattern Sheet B. Cut out the pieces following the instructions listed on the templates.

LAYOUT DIAGRAM

TOP (make 2 symmetrical tops)

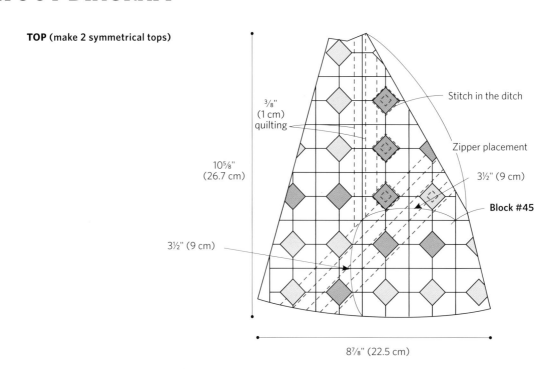

³⁄₈" (1 cm) quilting

10⅝" (26.7 cm)

3½" (9 cm)

Stitch in the ditch

Zipper placement

3½" (9 cm)

Block #45

8⅞" (22.5 cm)

BOTTOM

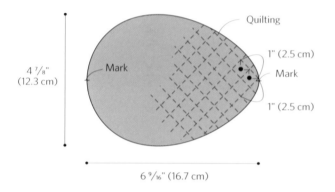

Quilting

Mark

Mark

1" (2.5 cm)

1" (2.5 cm)

4 ⁷⁄₈" (12.3 cm)

6 ⁹⁄₁₆" (16.7 cm)

» Stitch in the ditch around all patchwork pieces.

» Sew using ¼" (0.6 cm) seam allowance, unless otherwise noted.

HANDLE (cut 1 of each fabric on the bias)

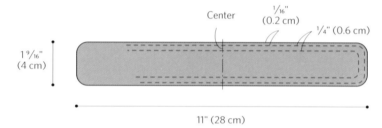

Center

¹⁄₁₆" (0.2 cm)

¼" (0.6 cm)

1 ⁹⁄₁₆" (4 cm)

11" (28 cm)

MAKE THE TOPS

1 Follow the instructions on page 94 to make 16 of Block #45. To make each top, sew eight blocks together into one row of two and two rows of three. Make sure the tops are symmetrical.

2 Make a template of the top and mark the finishing lines. Make sure to use the reverse side of the template for one of the tops in order to create two symmetrical tops. Cut out the tops, leaving a large seam allowance.

3 Cut the battings and backings slightly larger than the assembled tops. Layer each batting, backing, and top with right sides together. Sew together along the side where the zipper will be attached. Trim the batting seam allowances and turn right side out.

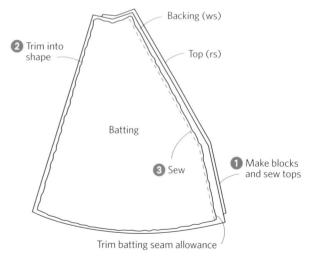

Make two symmetrical tops

Backing (ws)

2 Trim into shape

Top (rs)

Batting

3 Sew

1 Make blocks and sew tops

Trim batting seam allowance

SEW THE TOPS TOGETHER

1. Baste each top along the outer edges.

2. Quilt, as shown in the Layout Diagram on page 96.

3. Align the two tops with right sides together. Whipstitch together underneath where the zipper will be attached.

4. Sew one side of the zipper to each top using a ¼" (0.6 cm) seam allowance. Fold the raw edges of the zipper under and slip-stitch to the backing. Trim excess zipper length if necessary.

5. Align the two tops with right sides together and sew along the side.

6. Trim all seam allowances, except one of the backings, to ¼" (0.6 cm).

7. Wrap the backing seam allowance around the trimmed seam allowance and slip-stitch.

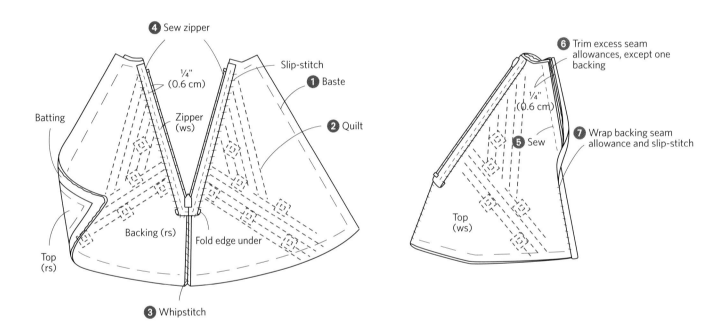

MAKE THE BOTTOM

1. Adhere heavyweight fusible interfacing to the wrong side of the bottom foundation.

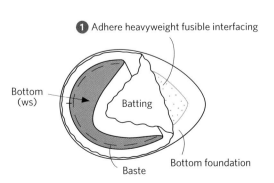

MAKE THE BOTTOM (continued)

② Layer bottom, batting, and bottom foundation. Baste, then quilt, as shown in the Layout Diagram on page 97.

③ Running stitch the bag along the bottom outline and gather into shape. Align the bottom and the bag with right sides together and sew.

④ Adhere heavyweight fusible interfacing to the wrong side of the bottom lining.

⑤ Running stitch the bottom lining and gather into shape.

⑥ Slip-stitch the bottom lining to the inside of the bag.

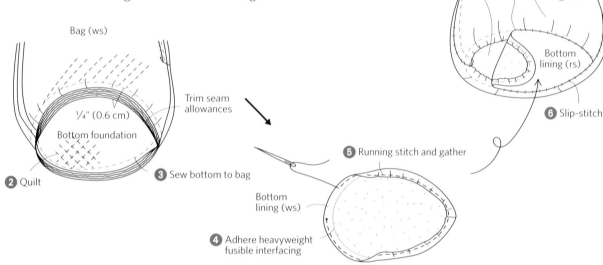

Bag (ws)

Trim seam allowances

¼" (0.6 cm)

Bottom foundation

② Quilt

③ Sew bottom to bag

Bottom lining (ws)

④ Adhere heavyweight fusible interfacing

⑤ Running stitch and gather

Bottom foundation

Bag (ws)

Bottom lining (rs)

⑥ Slip-stitch

MAKE THE HANDLE

① Adhere heavyweight fusible interfacing to the wrong side of one handle.

② Layer the batting and the handles with right sides together. Sew, leaving a 5 ⅛" (13 cm) opening to turn right side out.

③ Trim the excess batting seam allowance and turn right side out. Slip-stitch the opening closed.

④ Topstitch the handle around the outer edges.

⑤ Fold the handle in half widthwise and slip-stitch the long edges together for 7" (18 cm) along the center.

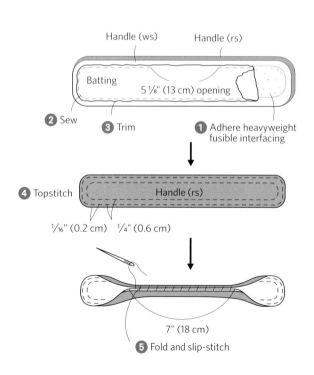

Handle (ws)   Handle (rs)

Batting

5 ⅛" (13 cm) opening

② Sew   **③** Trim   **①** Adhere heavyweight fusible interfacing

④ Topstitch   Handle (rs)

1/16" (0.2 cm)   ¼" (0.6 cm)

7" (18 cm)

⑤ Fold and slip-stitch

ATTACH THE HANDLE

1. Align handle with bag and sew, stitching through the inner layer of the handle only, so the stitches are not visible on the outside.

2. Backstitch on the handle topstitching to secure handle ends to bag. Stitch through all layers.

3. Slip-stitch handle ends to bag.

4. Slip-stitch handle ends together.

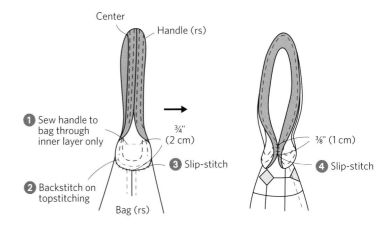

Center

Handle (rs)

1 Sew handle to bag through inner layer only

¾" (2 cm)

3 Slip-stitch

2 Backstitch on topstitching

Bag (rs)

⅜" (1 cm)

4 Slip-stitch

MAKE THE ZIPPER CHARM

1. Fold the cord in half and tie to the zipper pull. Thread the wooden bead onto the cord and knot.

2. Press in the raw edges of a small scrap so the piece is about ¼" (0.6 cm) wide. Fold the piece in half, covering the knot, and slip-stitch.

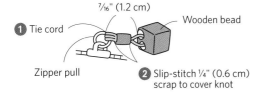

⁷⁄₁₆" (1.2 cm)

1 Tie cord

Wooden bead

Zipper pull

2 Slip-stitch ¼" (0.6 cm) scrap to cover knot

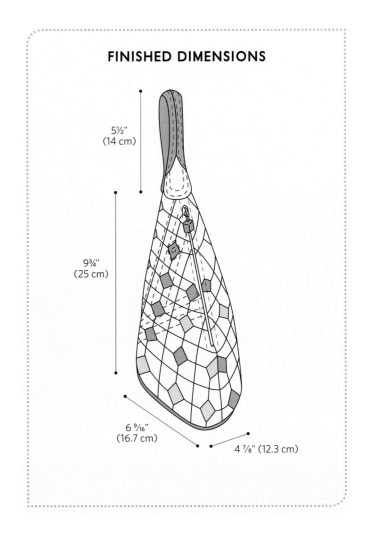

FINISHED DIMENSIONS

5½" (14 cm)

9¾" (25 cm)

6 ⁹⁄₁₆" (16.7 cm)

4 ⅞" (12.3 cm)

CONSTRUCTION STEPS

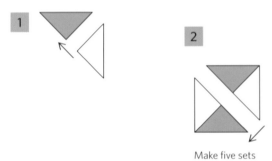

Make five sets

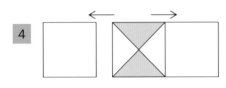

Make two sets

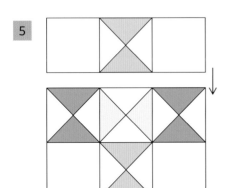

» When cutting your fabric, add ¼" (0.6 cm) seam allowance around each patchwork piece.
» When adjacent pieces are divided with a gray line, use the same fabric.
» Always press the seam allowances in the direction indicated by the arrows.

46 Nova

The classic variable star quilt motif is transformed in this simple block. I used a dark and light color combination to emphasize contrast within this block. I find it so interesting that a common design can be reinvented just by changing the fabric colors.

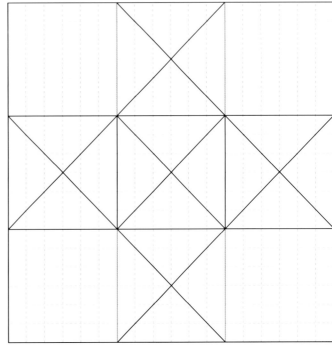

47 Shade of a Tree

A pair of sawtooth borders flank a simple diamond motif and create this pine tree-inspired block. The thin black strips elongate the block and accentuate the contrast between the dark green and light green fabrics.

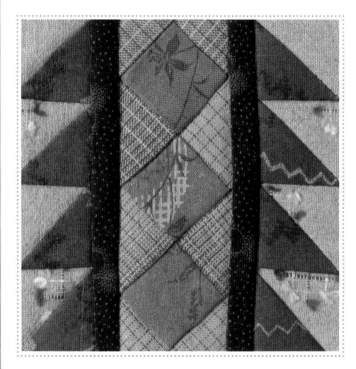

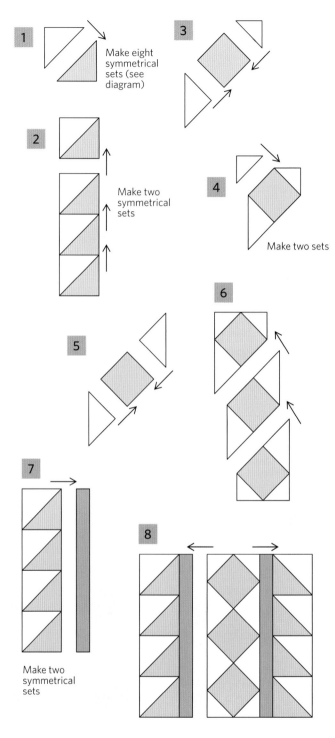

1 Make eight symmetrical sets (see diagram)

2 Make two symmetrical sets

4 Make two sets

7 Make two symmetrical sets

» When cutting your fabric, add ¼" (0.6 cm) seam allowance around each patchwork piece.

» When adjacent pieces are divided with a gray line, use the same fabric.

» Always press the seam allowances in the direction indicated by the arrows.

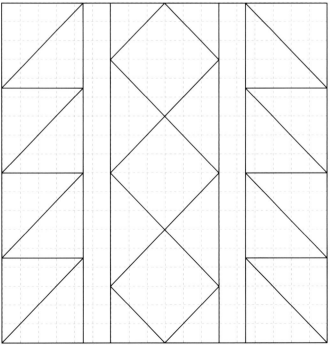

CONSTRUCTION STEPS

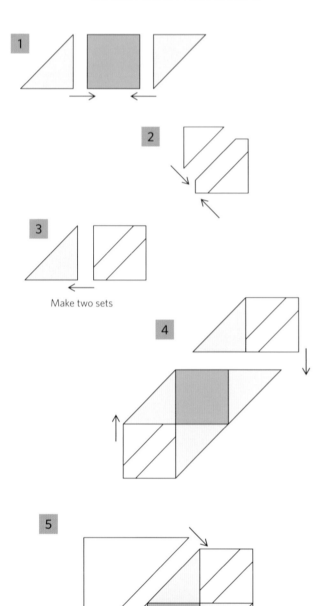

1

2

3

Make two sets

4

5

48 Flying Knot

Position repeats of this block at different angles to create a contemporary and dynamic quilt. Since the thin, ribbon-like strip divides this design on the diagonal, choose a fabric that complements the pattern as a whole.

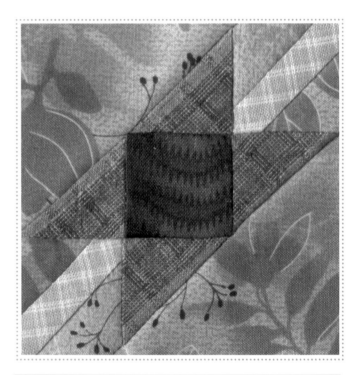

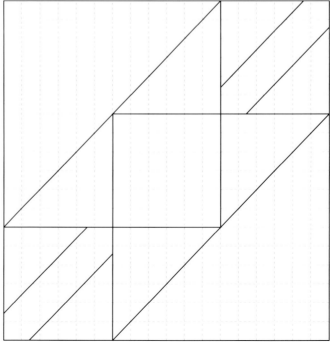

» When cutting your fabric, add ¼" (0.6 cm) seam allowance around each patchwork piece.

» When adjacent pieces are divided with a gray line, use the same fabric.

» Always press the seam allowances in the direction indicated by the arrows.

49 Satellite

Just like the Flying Knot block on the previous page, this motif is also positioned on an angle. I used fabrics in a similar tone for the four triangles which comprise the central square.
For a variation on this design, make the central square out of fabrics that contrast with the surrounding patchwork pieces.

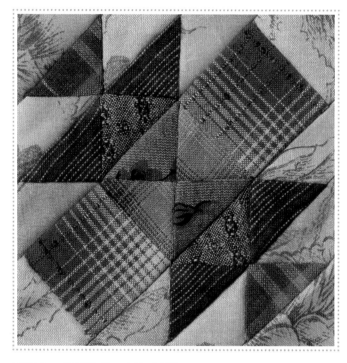

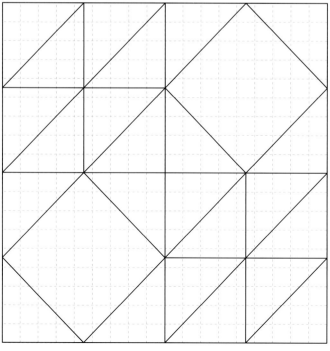

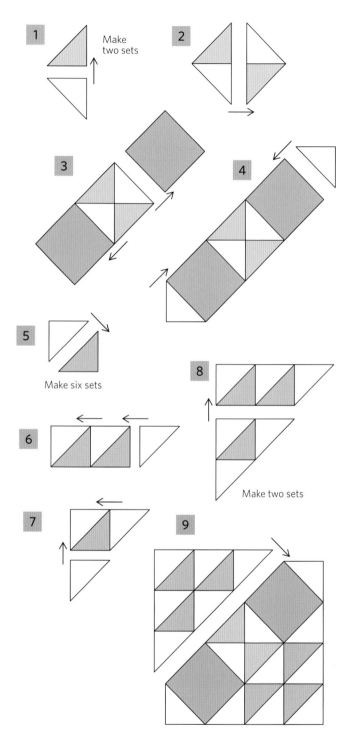

» When cutting your fabric, add ¼" (0.6 cm) seam allowance around each patchwork piece.
» When adjacent pieces are divided with a gray line, use the same fabric.
» Always press the seam allowances in the direction indicated by the arrows.

CONSTRUCTION STEPS

1 Make twelve sets

2 Make two sets

3

4

Make another set using white for both end triangles

5

6

» When cutting your fabric, add ¼" (0.6 cm) seam allowance around each patchwork piece.

» When adjacent pieces are divided with a gray line, use the same fabric.

» Always press the seam allowances in the direction indicated by the arrows.

50 Sawtooth Basket

This motif is a slight variation of the traditional sawtooth basket quilt block. I simply replaced the bottom triangle of the basket with background fabric to change the balance and create a fresh new look.

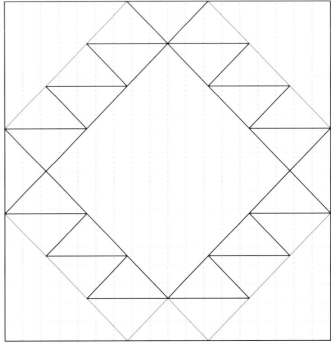

51 Simplicity

This sweet and simple block combines two basic shapes: squares and triangles. For the top and bottom squares of this motif, I chose a taupe fabric similar in tone to the background fabric. If you want to make the four-patch pattern more noticeable, use a fabric in a contrasting color.

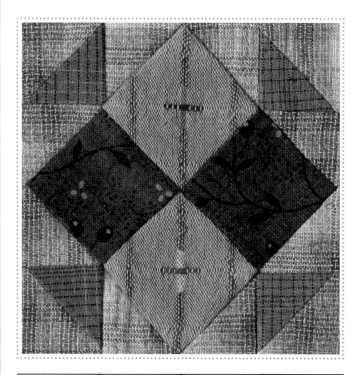

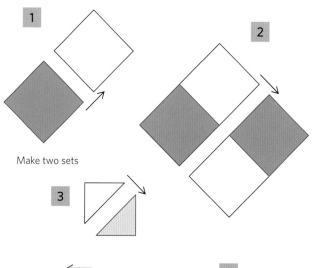

1

2

Make two sets

3

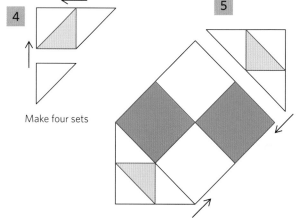

4

Make four sets

5

6

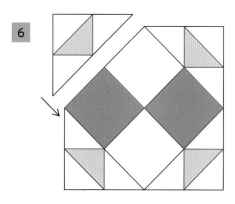

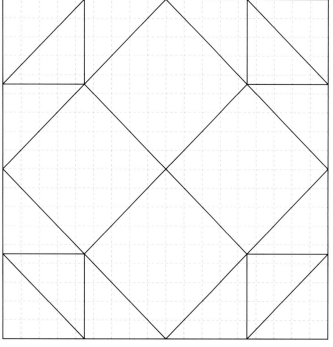

» When cutting your fabric, add ¼" (0.6 cm) seam allowance around each patchwork piece.

» When adjacent pieces are divided with a gray line, use the same fabric.

» Always press the seam allowances in the direction indicated by the arrows.

CONSTRUCTION STEPS

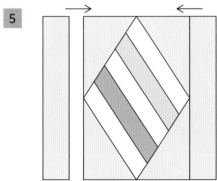

Positioning the rhombus in the center of this block creates negative space on both sides. You can change the feel of this design by the positioning the rhombus horizontally instead of vertically.

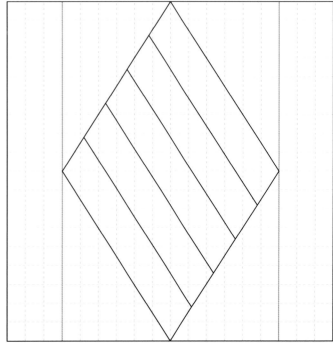

» When cutting your fabric, add ¼" (0.6 cm) seam allowance around each patchwork piece.
» When adjacent pieces are divided with a gray line, use the same fabric.
» Always press the seam allowances in the direction indicated by the arrows.

53 Spindle

The direction of this spindle-like rhombus can be changed depending on how you plan to use the motif. If following the color scheme pictured here, make sure to use a darker fabric for the left half of the block background to ensure visual balance.

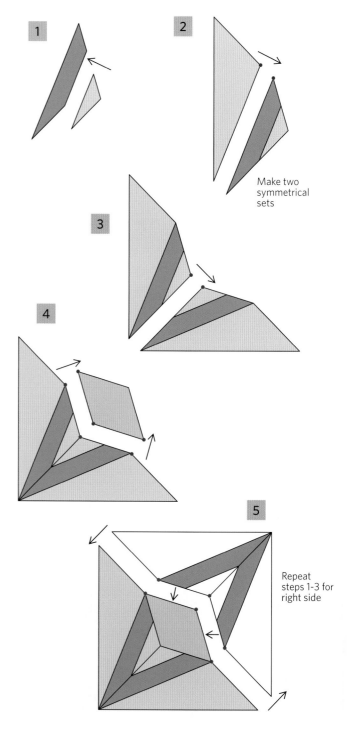

Make two symmetrical sets

Repeat steps 1–3 for right side

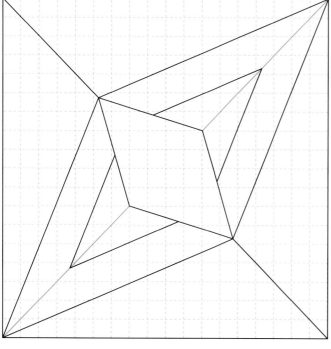

» When cutting your fabric, add ¼" (0.6 cm) seam allowance around each patchwork piece.

» When adjacent pieces are divided with a gray line, use the same fabric.

» Always press the seam allowances in the direction indicated by the arrows.

» The • marks to stop sewing at the seam allowance.

CONSTRUCTION STEPS

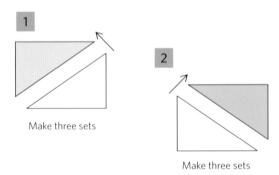

1

Make three sets

2

Make three sets

3

4

5

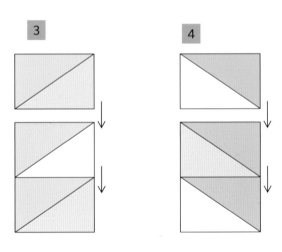

» When cutting your fabric, add ¼" (0.6 cm) seam allowance around each patchwork piece.

» When adjacent pieces are divided with a gray line, use the same fabric.

» Always press the seam allowances in the direction indicated by the arrows.

54 Triangles

This block is my interpretation of the famous flying geese motif. In this version, I used different prints in the same color tone for each triangle and background to add depth and dimension. Because this design is simple, it looks great when combined with other patchwork blocks and works especially well as a border motif.

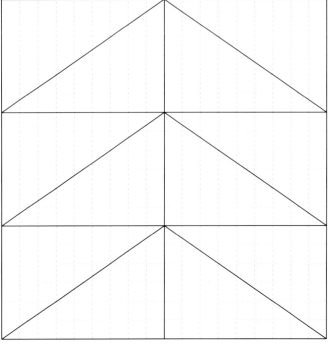

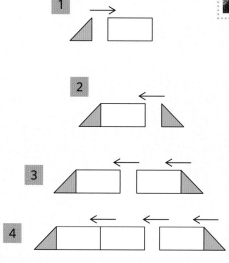

55 Stacked Pyramids

This pyramid motif is constructed by stacking brick-shaped pieces on top of each other. I used a dark, nearly solid fabric for the triangular backgrounds to allow the colorful rectangular blocks to stand out.

» When cutting your fabric, add ¼" (0.6 cm) seam allowance around each patchwork piece.

» When adjacent pieces are divided with a gray line, use the same fabric.

» Always press the seam allowances in the direction indicated by the arrows.

CONSTRUCTION STEPS

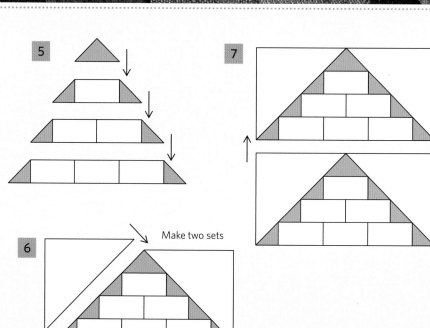

Make two sets

CONSTRUCTION STEPS

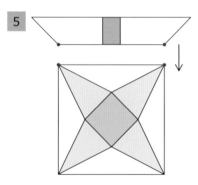

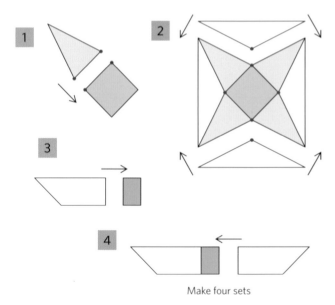

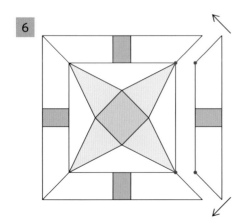

Make four sets

I inserted pieces of background fabric between the dark rectangles and the inner portion of this motif to allow the gem-like motif to truly shine. The seams used to piece this block together replicate the facets of a gem stone and add visual interest.

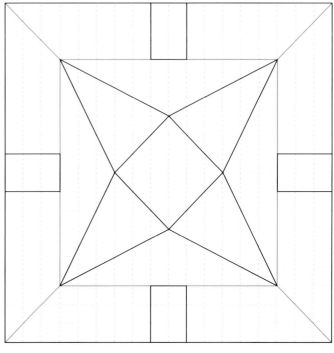

» When cutting your fabric, add ¼" (0.6 cm) seam allowance around each patchwork piece.

» When adjacent pieces are divided with a gray line, use the same fabric.

» Always press the seam allowances in the direction indicated by the arrows.

» The • marks to stop sewing at the seam allowance.

CONSTRUCTION STEPS

57 Triangle Puzzle

Inspired by the classic card trick motif, this block contains a series of six overlapping triangular sections. An optical illusion is at work in this block: use contrasting colors, then watch the small triangles morph into two larger intertwined triangles!

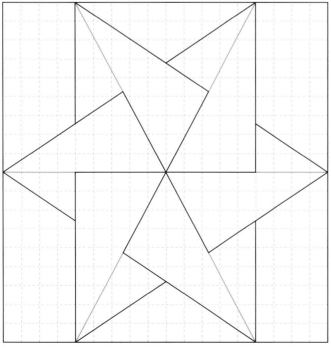

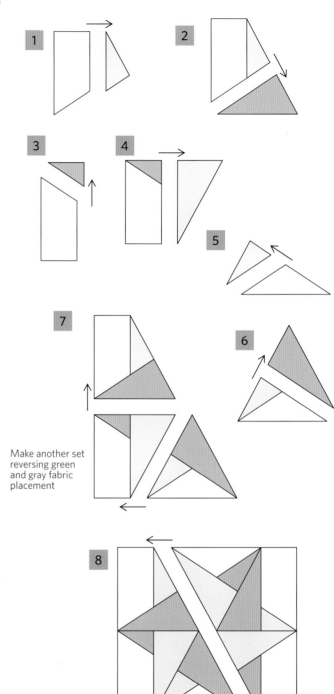

Make another set reversing green and gray fabric placement

» When cutting your fabric, add ¼" (0.6 cm) seam allowance around each patchwork piece.

» When adjacent pieces are divided with a gray line, use the same fabric.

» Always press the seam allowances in the direction indicated by the arrows.

CONSTRUCTION STEPS

1

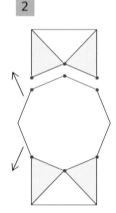

Make four sets

2

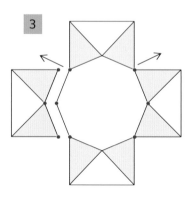

3

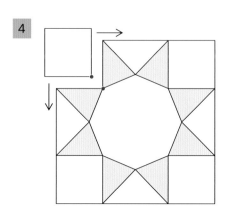

4

» When cutting your fabric, add ¼" (0.6 cm) seam allowance around each patchwork piece.

» When adjacent pieces are divided with a gray line, use the same fabric.

» Always press the seam allowances in the direction indicated by the arrows.

» The • marks to stop sewing at the seam allowance.

58 Coronet

Construct this circular crown motif by piecing eight small triangles around a large octagon. By limiting myself to just two fabrics, I was able to achieve a simple, yet striking design.

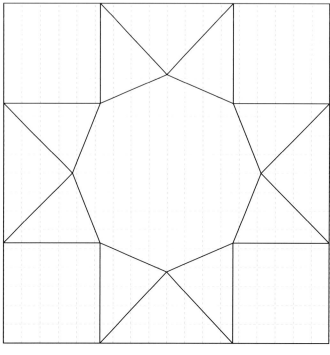

59 Geometric Daisy

This eye-catching design started with a patchwork star, then I added square blocks to form a large, rounded flower. While black and green fabrics are used here, this block works in just about any color combination. If you use green for the square pieces, it will look as if the flower is surrounded by leaves.

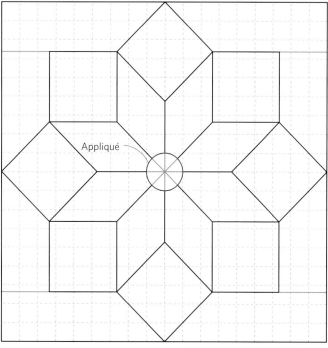

Appliqué

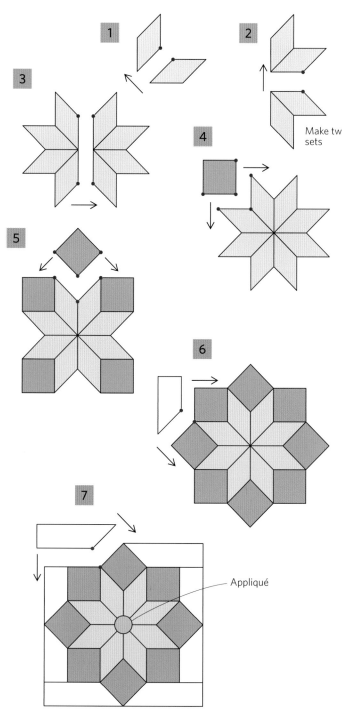

Make two sets

Appliqué

» When cutting your fabric, add ¼" (0.6 cm) seam allowance around each patchwork piece.
» When adjacent pieces are divided with a gray line, use the same fabric.
» Always press the seam allowances in the direction indicated by the arrows.
» The • marks to stop sewing at the seam allowance.

CONSTRUCTION STEPS

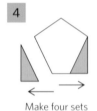

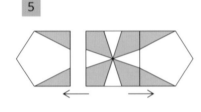

Make two sets

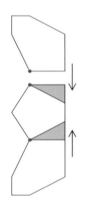 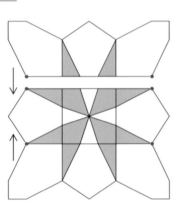

Make four sets

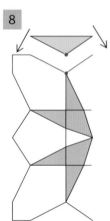

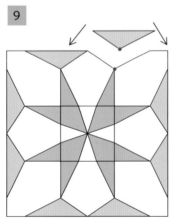

» When cutting your fabric, add ¼" (0.6 cm) seam allowance around each patchwork piece.

» When adjacent pieces are divided with a gray line, use the same fabric.

» Always press the seam allowances in the direction indicated by the arrows.

» The • marks to stop sewing at the seam allowance.

60 Four Petals

Contrast plays a starring role in the design of this block. To make the motif stand out, I positioned a dark, nearly solid flower on a light, patterned background fabric. As a finishing touch, I added small triangles along the outer edges, which emphasize the zigzag shape of the background pieces.

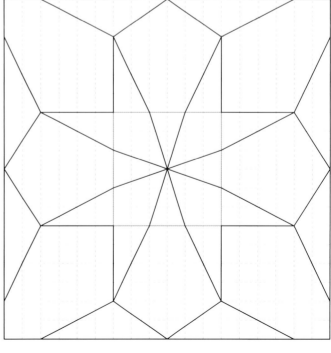

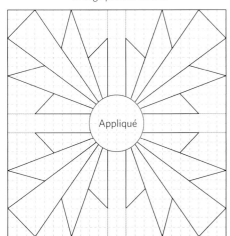

61 Cornflower

This cornflower design was created with a combination of patchwork and appliqué techniques. Make four identical blocks and sew them together with background fabric pieces sandwiched in between. The center circle is sewn using appliqué. The combination of finely divided pieces resembles the sharp petals of a cornflower.

CONSTRUCTION STEPS

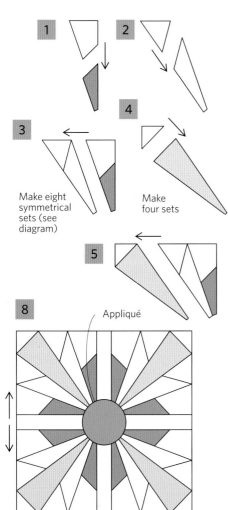

Make eight symmetrical sets (see diagram)

Make four sets

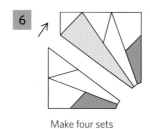

Make four sets

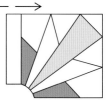

» When cutting your fabric, add ¼" (0.6 cm) seam allowance around each patchwork piece.

» When adjacent pieces are divided with a gray line, use the same fabric.

» Always press the seam allowances in the direction indicated by the arrows.

CONSTRUCTION STEPS

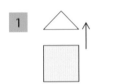 1

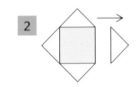 2

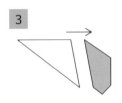 3

 4

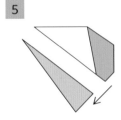 5

 6

Make four sets

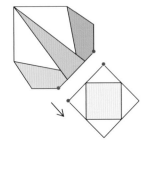 7

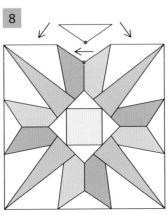 8

» When cutting your fabric, add ¼" (0.6 cm) seam allowance around each patchwork piece.
» When adjacent pieces are divided with a gray line, use the same fabric.
» Always press the seam allowances in the direction indicated by the arrows.
» The • marks to stop sewing at the seam allowance.

62 Twinkling Star

Several sharp, thin pieces combine to form this stunning star. Believe it or not, I used six different fabrics in this block. I think the combination of different colors and prints makes this patchwork star all the more unique.

63 Star Cross

A star is born! This motif combines a cross made of five squares with triangle and rhombus pieces. Five different fabrics are used here, yet their neutral color palette prevents the block from becoming too busy.

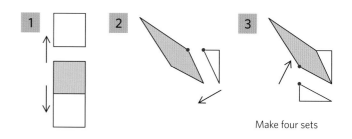

Make four sets

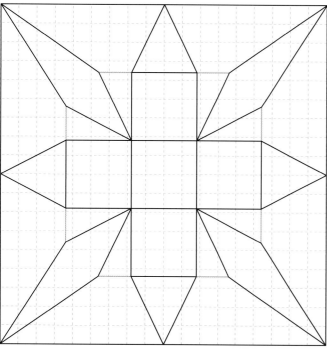

Make two sets

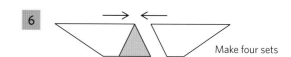

Make four sets

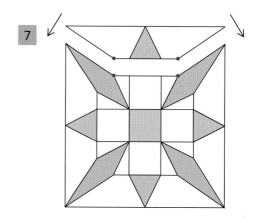

» When cutting your fabric, add ¼" (0.6 cm) seam allowance around each patchwork piece.

» When adjacent pieces are divided with a gray line, use the same fabric.

» Always press the seam allowances in the direction indicated by the arrows.

» The • marks to stop sewing at the seam allowance.

CONSTRUCTION STEPS

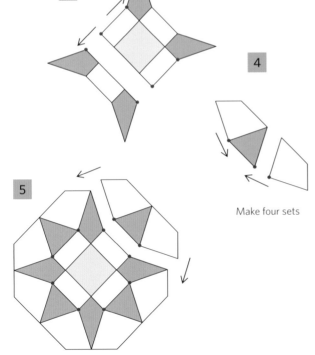

Make two sets

Make four sets

64 Shining Star

A stocky little cross is framed by a large, bold star in this sparkling design. The beige background pieces seem as if they've been cut off at the edge of the block, creating the impression that this star is stretching out its arms.

» When cutting your fabric, add ¼" (0.6 cm) seam allowance around each patchwork piece.

» When adjacent pieces are divided with a gray line, use the same fabric.

» Always press the seam allowances in the direction indicated by the arrows.

» The • marks to stop sewing at the seam allowance.

65 Far Off Star

This pattern exclusively uses a combination of taupe fabrics, creating the "far off" effect. If you use striped or plaid fabric as pictured here, pay attention to the orientation of the patterns. Even if the individual pieces are small, their orientation can have a big impact on the look and feel of the completed block.

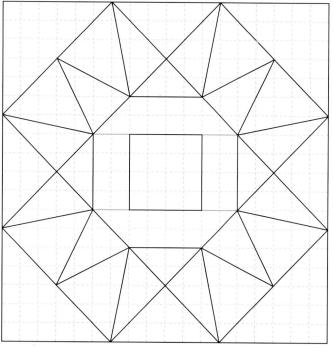

CONSTRUCTION STEPS

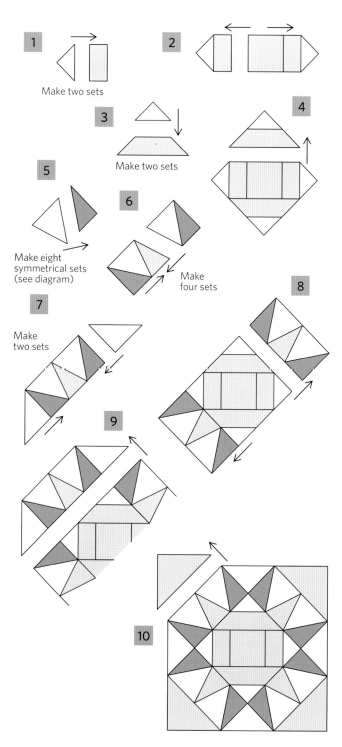

» When cutting your fabric, add ¼" (0.6 cm) seam allowance around each patchwork piece.

» When adjacent pieces are divided with a gray line, use the same fabric.

» Always press the seam allowances in the direction indicated by the arrows.

CONSTRUCTION STEPS

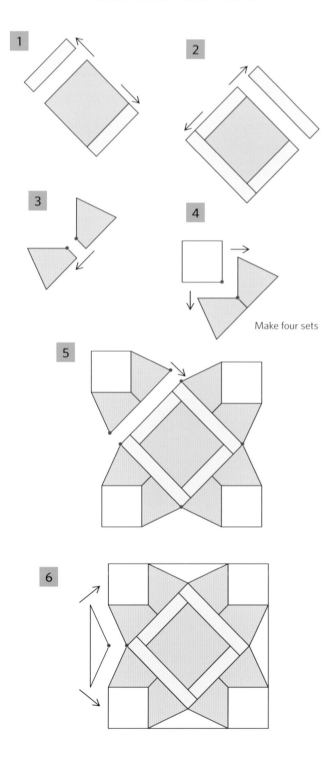

66 Eight Point Star

At first glance, this may look like a simple block composed of triangles and squares. Look closely and you'll notice that the star points are actually made of irregularly-shaped quadrilaterals, not triangles. This minor detail creates a star with a softer overall impression.

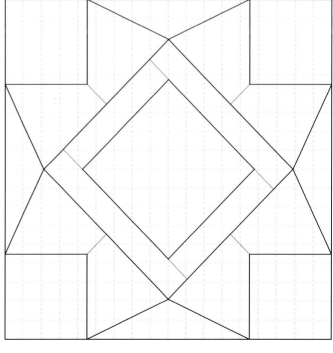

Make four sets

» When cutting your fabric, add ¼" (0.6 cm) seam allowance around each patchwork piece.

» When adjacent pieces are divided with a gray line, use the same fabric.

» Always press the seam allowances in the direction indicated by the arrows.

» The • marks to stop sewing at the seam allowance.

Enlarge pattern 200%

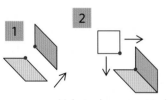

67 Desert Rose

This block features a traditional LeMoyne star surrounded by four half star motifs. The shapes and colors used in this design remind me of a desert rose growing in a dusty square of earth. Because this block contains so many small pieces, I decided to make it slightly larger than most of the other blocks in the book.

» When cutting your fabric, add ¼" (0.6 cm) seam allowance around each patchwork piece.
» When adjacent pieces are divided with a gray line, use the same fabric.
» Always press the seam allowances in the direction indicated by the arrows.
» The • marks to stop sewing at the seam allowance.

CONSTRUCTION STEPS

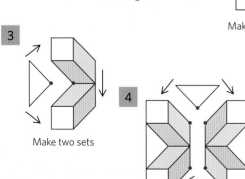

Make twelve symmetrical sets using different fabric combinations (see diagram)

Make four sets

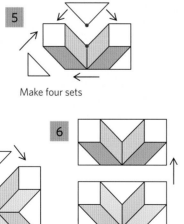

Make two sets

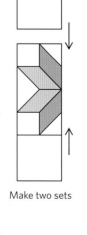

Make two sets

Make two sets

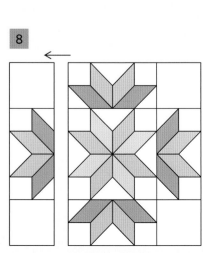

CONSTRUCTION STEPS

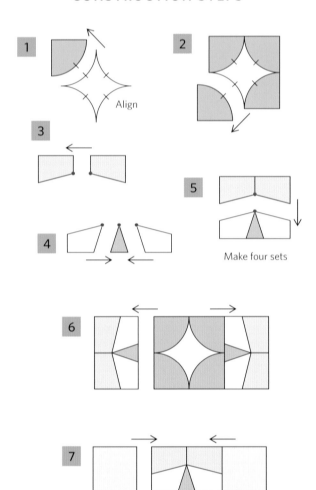

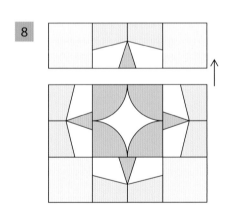

This block incorporates curves, giving it a softer appearance and setting it apart from other star motifs, which tend to have sharp, pointed shapes. I positioned the star in the middle of a neutral-colored cross to further accentuate the airiness of this design.

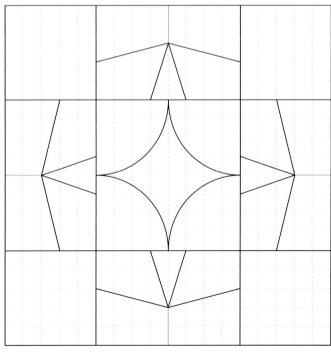

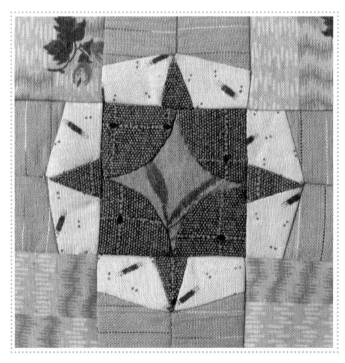

» When cutting your fabric, add ¼" (0.6 cm) seam allowance around each patchwork piece.

» When adjacent pieces are divided with a gray line, use the same fabric.

» Always press the seam allowances in the direction indicated by the arrows.

» The • marks to stop sewing at the seam allowance.

69 Twist and Turn

This motif may appear to be slanted; however, the horizontal line is actually parallel to the edge of this block. This slightly off balance design is sure to catch the eye, especially when constructed from materials with interesting directional patterns. For added movement, use a checkered background fabric.

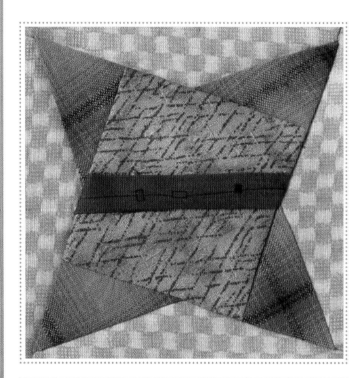

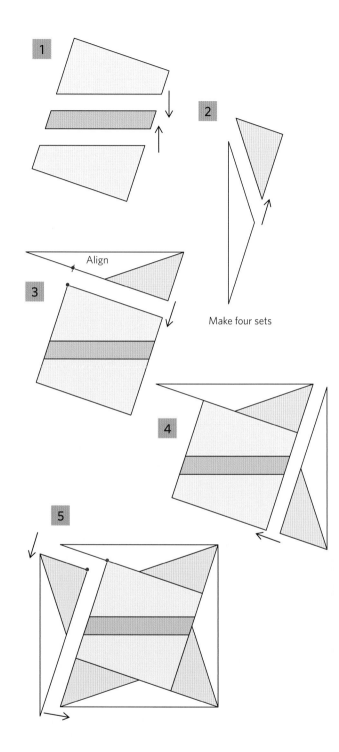

Align

Make four sets

» When cutting your fabric, add ¼" (0.6 cm) seam allowance around each patchwork piece.
» When adjacent pieces are divided with a gray line, use the same fabric.
» Always press the seam allowances in the direction indicated by the arrows.
» The • marks to stop sewing at the seam allowance.

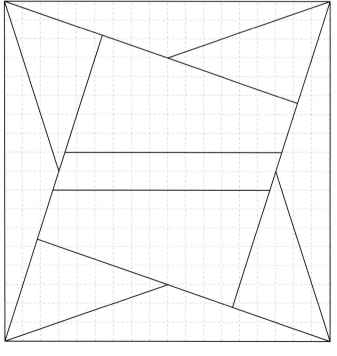

CONSTRUCTION STEPS

1

2

3

4

5

6

7

8

Make four sets using different fabrics

9

10

70 Freehand Squares

The squares in this block look as if they were drawn by hand. Use a medium toned background fabric to make the squares pop. This block inspired the Freehand Squares Pouch on page 126.

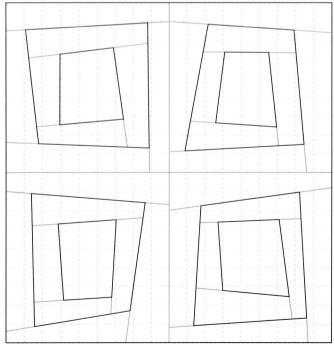

» When cutting your fabric, add ¼" (0.6 cm) seam allowance around each patchwork piece.

» When adjacent pieces are divided with a gray line, use the same fabric.

» Always press the seam allowances in the direction indicated by the arrows.

Freehand Squares Pouch

This rounded pouch includes mitered corners, so it's sturdy and can hold quite a lot. It uses the **Freehand Squares** block shown on page 125, as well as a fun zigzag appliqué positioned along the top. To keep the look cohesive, I used the same assortment of fabrics for the zigzag appliqué as I used for the squares.

Instructions on page 127

MATERIALS FOR FREE-HAND SQUARES POUCH

Patchwork and appliqué fabric: Assorted scraps

Main fabric: 11¾" × 19¾" (30 × 50 cm) brown print

Backing: 11¾" × 15¾" (30 × 40 cm)

Batting: 11¾" × 15¾" (30 × 40 cm)

Binding:

    For pouch opening: Two 1⅜" × 7⅞" (3.5 × 20 cm) green striped bias strips

    For seam allowances: One 1³⁄₁₆" × 19¾" (3 × 50 cm) bias strip

Fusible interfacing: ¾" × 2¾" (2 × 7 cm)

Zipper: One 6" (15 cm) long zipper

Cord: 2⅜" (6 cm) of ¹⁄₃₂" (0.1 cm) diameter cord

Bead: One square wooden bead

CUTTING INSTRUCTIONS

Seam allowance is not included. Add ¼" (0.6 cm) seam allowance to all piece edges.

Trace and cut out the Block #70 template on page 125 and the template on Pattern Sheet B. Cut out the pieces following the instructions listed on the templates.

Cut out the following pieces, which do not have templates, according to the measurements below:

» **Tabs (cut 2 on the bias without seam allowance):** 1¹⁄₁₆" × 2¾" (2.6 × 7 cm) of scrap fabric

» **Tab interfacings (cut 2 without seam allowance):** ⁵⁄₁₆" × 2¾" (0.9 × 7 cm) of fusible interfacing

LAYOUT DIAGRAM

TOP (make 2)

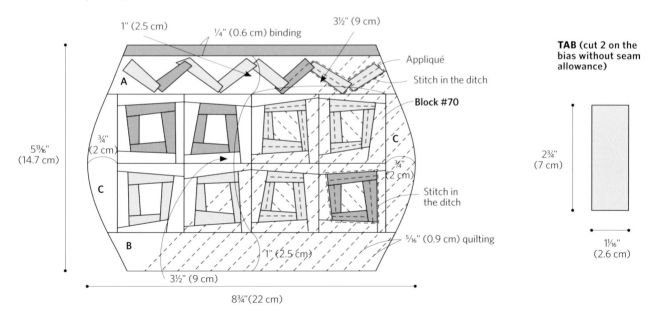

» Stitch in the ditch around all patchwork and appliqué pieces.

» Sew using ¼" (0.6 cm) seam allowance, unless otherwise noted.

MAKE THE TOPS

1. Follow the instructions on page 125 to make four of Block #70. To make each top, sew two blocks together, then attach pieces A-C.

2. Appliqué the zigzag design to each top.

3. Cut the battings and backings slightly larger than the assembled tops. Layer each top, batting, and backing. Baste, then quilt, as shown in the Layout Diagram on page 127.

4. Bind the top openings with bias strips.

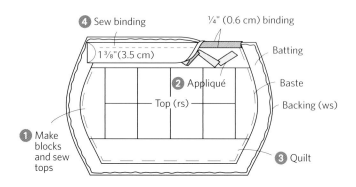

SEW THE POUCH TOGETHER

1. Align each side of the zipper with a top opening. Topstitch the binding to attach the zipper. Trim excess zipper length if necessary. Slip-stitch the zipper seam allowances to the backing.

2. Align the two tops with right sides together and sew along the bottom.

3. Trim all seam allowances, except for one backing, to ¼" (0.6 cm).

4. Wrap the backing seam allowance around the trimmed seam allowances and slip-stitch to the backing.

5. With the zipper open, sew the tops together along the sides.

6. With right sides together, sew bias strips to each side seam, leaving unattached along the lower 1³⁄₁₆" (3 cm). Wrap the bias strips around the seam allowances and slip-stitch.

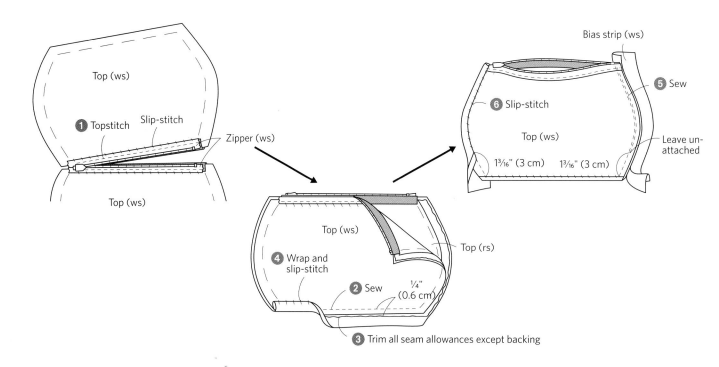

MAKE THE MITERED CORNERS

1. Refer to page 138 to make the mitered corners and finish the seam allowances.

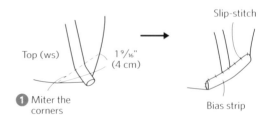

MAKE THE TABS

1. Adhere fusible interfacing to the wrong side of each tab.

2. Fold each tab in half with right sides together and sew. Press the seam allowances open. Turn right side out.

3. Center the seam allowances and topstitch the tabs.

4. Fold each tab in half and slip-stitch to the backing.

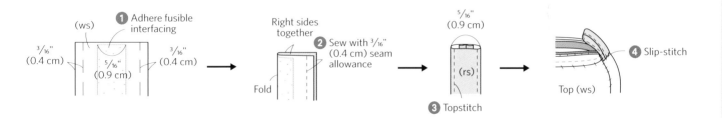

MAKE THE ZIPPER CHARM

1. Fold the cord in half and tie to the zipper pull. Thread the wooden bead onto the cord and knot.

2. Press in the raw edges of a small scrap, so the piece is about ⁵⁄₁₆" (0.9 cm) wide. Fold the piece in half, covering the knot, and slip-stitch.

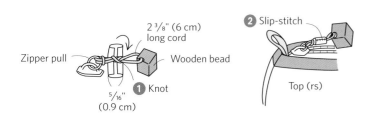

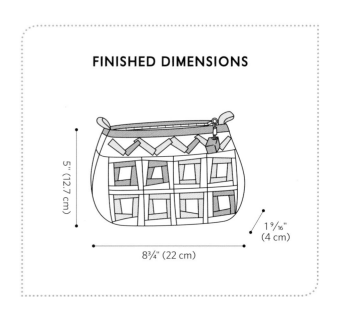

FINISHED DIMENSIONS

71 Framed Star

The inner portion of this motif is actually a rectangle, rather than a square. This unexpected variation may require the use of a few additional templates, but the finished product is well worth the effort!

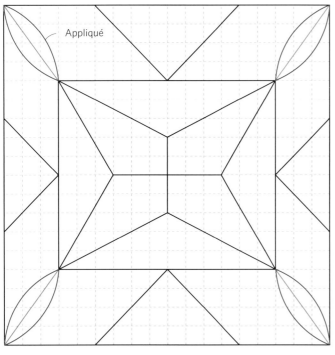

Appliqué

CONSTRUCTION STEPS

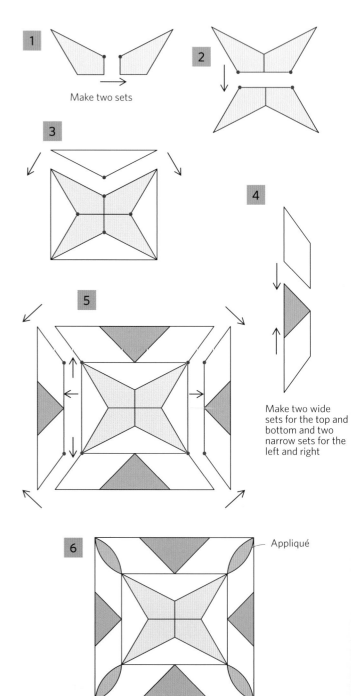

» When cutting your fabric, add ¼" (0.6 cm) seam allowance around each patchwork piece.

» When adjacent pieces are divided with a gray line, use the same fabric.

» Always press the seam allowances in the direction indicated by the arrows.

» The • marks to stop sewing at the seam allowance.

CONSTRUCTION STEPS

1

Make two symmetrical sets

2

3

Make two symmetrical sets

4

Make two symmetrical sets

5

Make two symmetrical sets

6

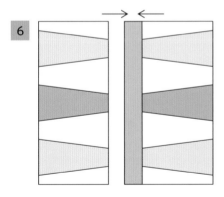

» When cutting your fabric, add ¼" (0.6 cm) seam allowance around each patchwork piece.

» When adjacent pieces are divided with a gray line, use the same fabric.

» Always press the seam allowances in the direction indicated by the arrows.

72 Kite Tail

This block features three brightly colored bows tied to a central vertical stripe—just like a classic kite tail. The vertical stripe is made from a checkered print and cut out on the bias.

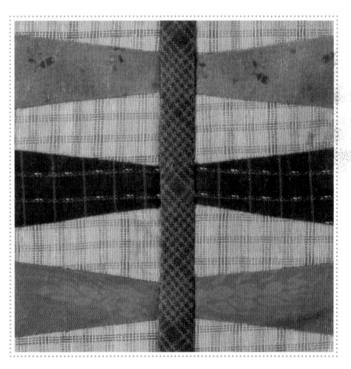

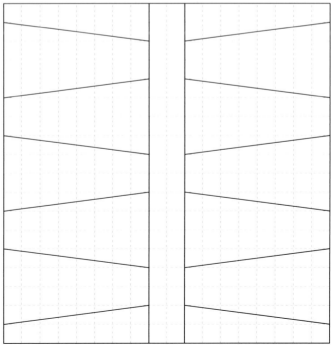

73 Classic Spool

The focal point of this block is one central spool motif. It is symmetrically positioned within the block, just touching each of the four small corner squares. If you use striped or plaid background fabric, be careful to cut the curved and rectangular pieces out in the same direction so the pattern looks continuous.

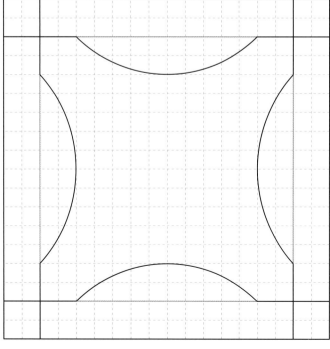

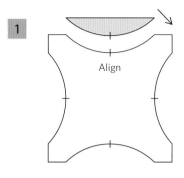

1 Align

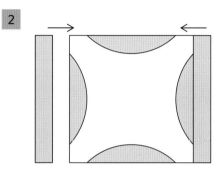

2

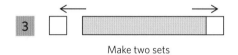

3 Make two sets

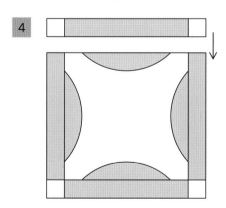

4

» When cutting your fabric, add ¼" (0.6 cm) seam allowance around each patchwork piece.
» When adjacent pieces are divided with a gray line, use the same fabric.
» Always press the seam allowances in the direction indicated by the arrows.

74 Native American Sun

This design was inspired by the beautiful textiles woven by Native Americans. In keeping with traditional style, I used red for the center and earth tones for the surrounding patchwork pieces. The long, narrow shape of this block makes it an ideal candidate for tapestry borders; however, it truly shines in the Sun Burst Tote featured on page 135.

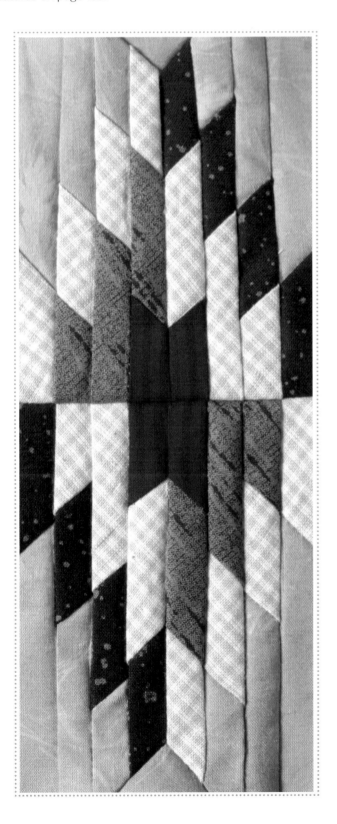

Enlarge pattern 200%

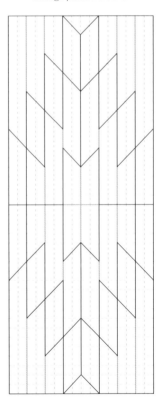

Construction steps on page 134.

CONSTRUCTION STEPS

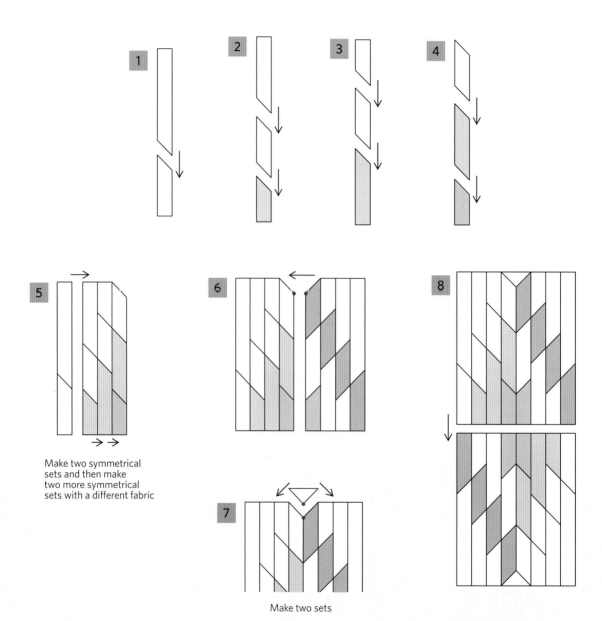

Make two symmetrical sets and then make two more symmetrical sets with a different fabric

Make two sets

» When cutting your fabric, add ¼" (0.6 cm) seam allowance around each patchwork piece.

» When adjacent pieces are divided with a gray line, use the same fabric.

» Always press the seam allowances in the direction indicated by the arrows.

» The • marks to stop sewing at the seam allowance.

Sun Burst Tote

Inspired by Native American rugs, this simply shaped bag showcases the large-scale graphic **Native American Sun** block. In this design, the quilting serves both decorative and functional purposes—it adds visual interest, as well as strength—making it the ideal bag for toting around your books or a laptop.

Instructions on page 136

MATERIALS FOR SUN BURST TOTE

Patchwork fabric: Five different scraps

Main fabric: 13¾" × 31½" (35 × 80 cm) dark brown stripe

Accent fabric: 9¾" × 13¾" (25 × 35 cm) brown checkered

Backing: 21¾" × 31½" (55 × 80 cm)

Batting: 21¾" × 31½" (55 × 80 cm)

Binding:

For bag opening: One 1⅜" × 78¾" (3.5 × 200 cm) dark brown corduroy bias strip

For seam allowances: Two 1" × 2⅜" (2.5 × 6 cm) bias strips

Nylon web tape: 18⅛" (46 cm) of 1⅜" (3.5 cm) wide dark brown nylon web tape

CUTTING INSTRUCTIONS

Seam allowance is not included. Add ¼" (0.6 cm) seam allowance to all piece edges.

Trace and cut out the Block #74 template on page 133. Cut out the pieces.

Cut out the following pieces, which do not have templates, according to the measurements below:

» **A (cut 4):** 2¾" × 11¾" (7 × 30 cm) of main fabric
» **B (cut 2):** 4¾" × 11¾" (12 × 30 cm) of main fabric
» **Borders (cut 8):** ⅜" × 11¾" (1 × 30 cm) of accent fabric

LAYOUT DIAGRAM

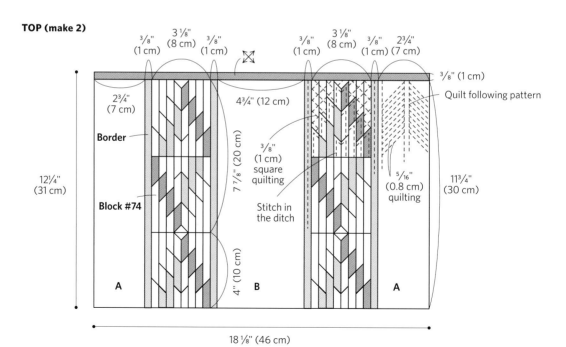

TOP (make 2)

» Stitch in the ditch around all patchwork pieces.
» Sew using ¼" (0.6 cm) seam allowance, unless otherwise noted.

MAKE THE TOPS

1 Follow the instruction on page 134 to make six of Block #74. For two of the blocks, leave the top and bottom halves separate. To make each top, sew the blocks together with the A, B, and border pieces, as shown in the Layout Diagram on page 136.

2 Cut the battings and backings slightly larger than the assembled tops. Layer each top, batting, and backing. Quilt, as shown in the Layout Diagram on page 136.

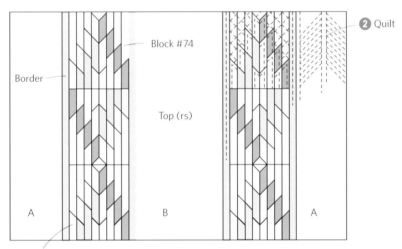

Block #74

Border

2 Quilt

Top (rs)

A

B

A

1 Make blocks and sew tops

SEW THE BAG TOGETHER

1 With right sides together, sew the two tops along the sides and bottom. Start and stop sewing ³⁄₈" (1 cm) beyond the finishing line.

2 Trim all seam allowances, except for one of the backings, to ¹⁄₄" (0.6 cm).

3 Wrap the backing seam allowance around the trimmed seam allowances and slip-stitch. Do not slip-stitch the backing seam allowance at the corners.

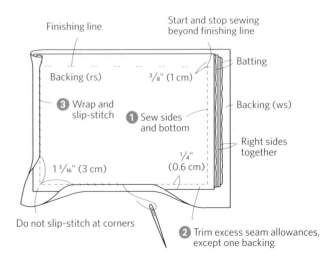

Finishing line

Start and stop sewing beyond finishing line

Batting

Backing (rs)

³⁄₈" (1 cm)

3 Wrap and slip-stitch

Backing (ws)

1 Sew sides and bottom

Right sides together

1³⁄₁₆" (3 cm)

¹⁄₄" (0.6 cm)

Do not slip-stitch at corners

2 Trim excess seam allowances, except one backing

MAKE THE MITERED CORNERS

1. On the wrong side of the bag, align the bottom and one of the side seams on top of each other. Sew across the corner with a 1⁹⁄₁₆" (4 cm) long seam perpendicular to the existing seams.

2. Sew a bias strip to the mitered corner seam.

3. Trim the excess seam allowances to ¼" (0.6 cm).

4. Fold in the long edge of the bias strip.

5. Fold in the short edges of the bias strip.

6. Wrap the bias strip around the trimmed seam allowances and slip-stitch to the backing. Repeat steps 1-6 for the other corner.

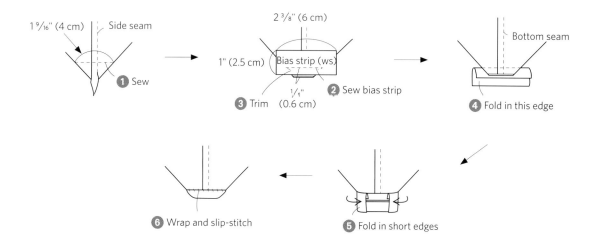

MAKE THE HANDLES

1. Cut the nylon web tape into two pieces, as shown in the diagram below. Fold each handle in half widthwise and sew the long edges together for 4¾" (12 cm) along the center.

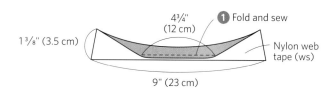

FINISH THE BAG

1 Baste the handles to the bag.

2 With right sides together, sew the bias strip to the bag opening. Overlap the short ends of the bias strip and sew together.

3 Trim the seam allowances to ¼" (0.6 cm).

4 Fold the bias strip so the right side is facing up. Topstitch the binding.

5 Wrap the bias strip around the trimmed seam allowances and slip-stitch to the backing.

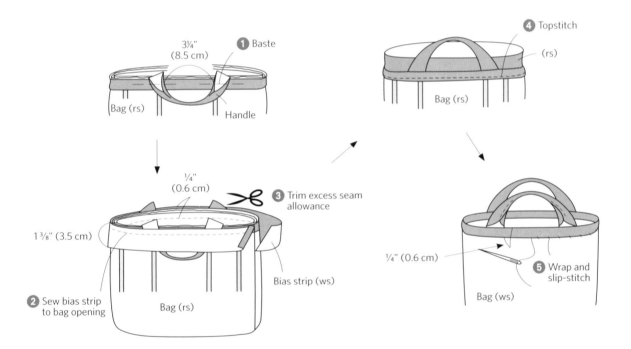

3¼"
(8.5 cm)

1 Baste

Bag (rs)

Handle

¼"
(0.6 cm)

3 Trim excess seam allowance

1 ⅜" (3.5 cm)

Bias strip (ws)

2 Sew bias strip to bag opening

Bag (rs)

4 Topstitch

(rs)

Bag (rs)

¼" (0.6 cm)

5 Wrap and slip-stitch

Bag (ws)

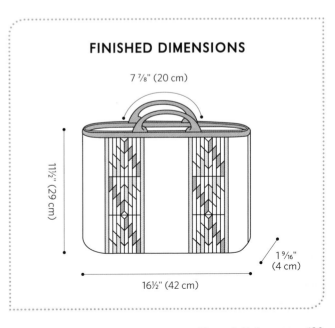

FINISHED DIMENSIONS

7 ⅞" (20 cm)

11½" (29 cm)

1 ⁹⁄₁₆"
(4 cm)

16½" (42 cm)

75 Polygon Flower

This block was inspired by the historic grandmother's flower garden motif. For my version, I swapped the traditional hexagon pieces for pentagons to create a star-shaped flower. Softly shaded background fabrics complete the block.

Enlarge pattern 200%

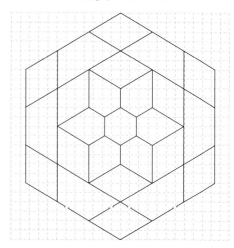

CONSTRUCTION STEPS

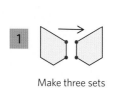

Make three sets

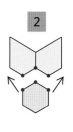

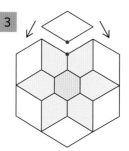

Make three sets

» When cutting your fabric, add ¼" (0.6 cm) seam allowance around each patchwork piece.

» When adjacent pieces are divided with a gray line, use the same fabric.

» Always press the seam allowances in the direction indicated by the arrows.

» The • marks to stop sewing at the seam allowance.

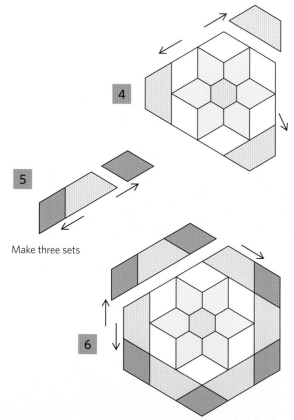

CONSTRUCTION STEPS

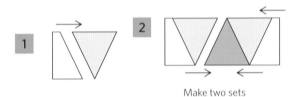

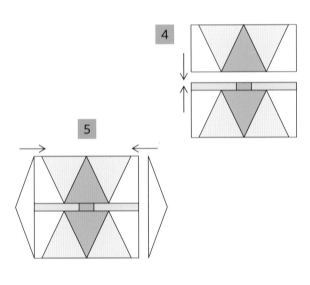

Make two sets

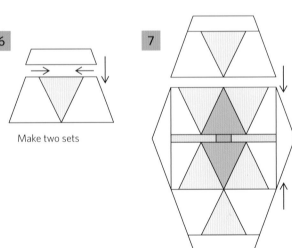

76 Dragon's Scale

Inspired by a knitting pattern, this large, irregularly-shaped hexagon block was designed to be used as a border. Align repeats of this motif vertically for a complex, detailed edging.

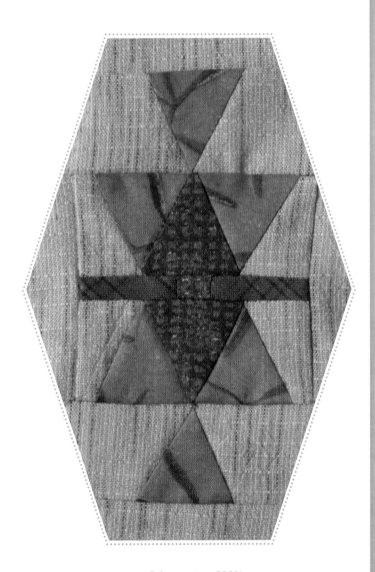

Enlarge pattern 200%

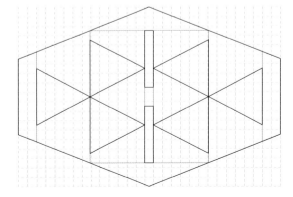

» When cutting your fabric, add ¼" (0.6 cm) seam allowance around each patchwork piece.

» When adjacent pieces are divided with a gray line, use the same fabric.

» Always press the seam allowances in the direction indicated by the arrows.

Make two sets

77 Playing Cards

This block reconfigures the card trick motif by aligning the pieces in a row. This design is ideal for borders and lattices, as you can connect as many blocks as you desire. For maximum impact, use different color fabrics for adjacent squares.

Enlarge pattern 200%

CONSTRUCTION STEPS

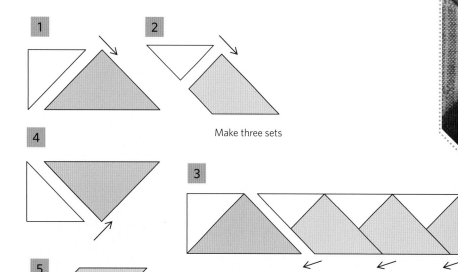

1

2

Make three sets

4

3

5

Make three sets

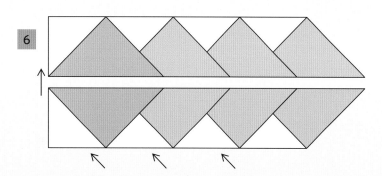

6

» When cutting your fabric, add ¼" (0.6 cm) seam allowance around each patchwork piece.

» When adjacent pieces are divided with a gray line, use the same fabric.

» Always press the seam allowances in the direction indicated by the arrows.

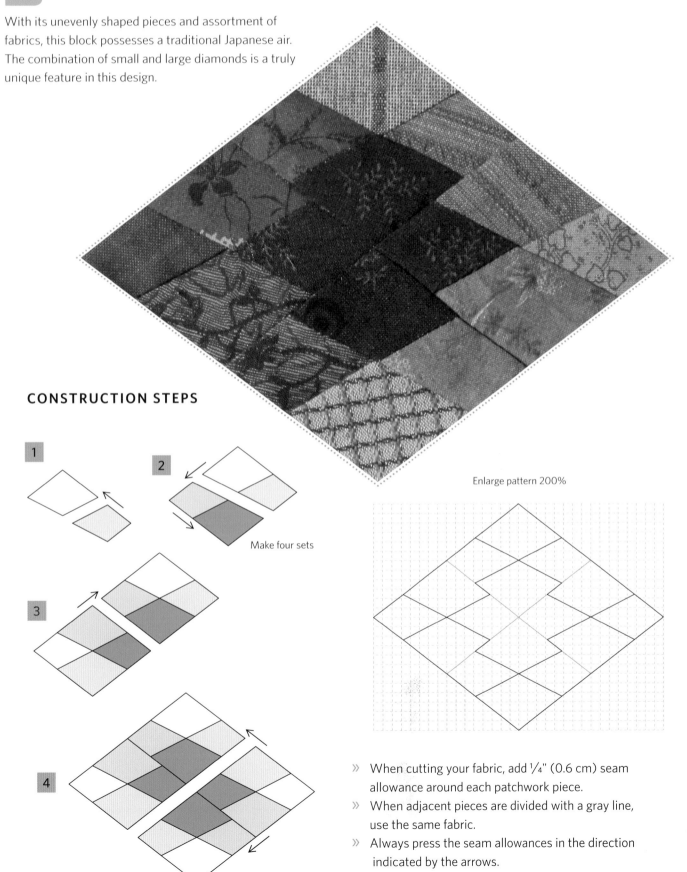

78 Rhombic Connection

With its unevenly shaped pieces and assortment of fabrics, this block possesses a traditional Japanese air. The combination of small and large diamonds is a truly unique feature in this design.

CONSTRUCTION STEPS

1

2

Make four sets

3

4

Enlarge pattern 200%

» When cutting your fabric, add ¼" (0.6 cm) seam allowance around each patchwork piece.

» When adjacent pieces are divided with a gray line, use the same fabric.

» Always press the seam allowances in the direction indicated by the arrows.

Looking for more Japanese-inspired quilting ideas?

Check out these great resources from Interweave

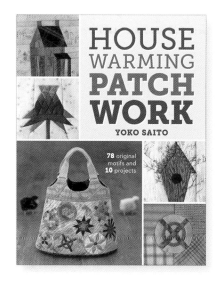

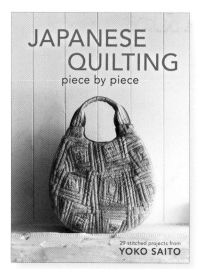

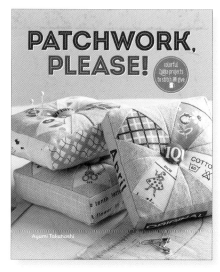

Housewarming Patchwork
78 Original Motifs and
10 Projects
Yoko Saito
ISBN 978-1-59668-819-3
$27.95

**Japanese Quilting
Piece by Piece**
29 Stitched Projects
from Yoko Saito
Yoko Saito
ISBN 978-1-59668-858-2
$26.95

Patchwork, Please!
Colorful Zakka Projects
to Stitch and Give
Ayumi Takahashi
ISBN 978-1-59668-599-4
$22.95

Available at your favorite retailer or

Quilting Daily Shop
shop.quiltingdaily.com

Quilting Arts MAGAZINE

Whether you consider yourself a contemporary quilter, fiber artist, art quilter, embellished quilter, or wearable art artist, *Quilting Arts Magazine* strives to meet your creative needs.
Quiltingdaily.com

Quilting Daily

Quiltingdaily.com, the online contemporary quilting community, offers free patterns, expert tips and techniques, e-newsletters, blogs, forums, videos, special offers, and more! **Quiltingdaily.com**